The European City

THE MAKING OF EUROPE
Series Editor: Jacques Le Goff

The Making of Europe series is the result of a unique collaboration between five European publishers – Beck in Germany, Blackwell in Great Britain and the United States, Critica in Spain, Laterza in Italy and le Seuil in France. Each book will be published in all five languages. The scope of the series is broad, encompassing the history of ideas as well as and including their interaction with the history of societies, nations, and states to produce informative, readable, and provocative treatments of central themes in the history of the European peoples and their cultures.

Published

The European City
Leonardo Benevolo

Europe and the Sea
Michel Mollat du Jourdin

European Revolutions, 1492–1992
Charles Tilly

In preparation

Literacy inEuropean History
Roger Chartier

Nature and the Culture of Europe
Robert Delort

The European Identity
Josep Fontana

The Enlightenment
Ulrich Im Hof

The Industrialization of Europe
Jordi Nadal

The Renaissance
Francisco Rico

The Peasantry of Europe
Werner Rosener

Divided Christendom
Peter Brown

The Romantic Movement
Maurice Cranston

The Perfect Language
Umberto Eco

The Individual in European History
Aaron Gurevitch

History and the Culture of Food
Massimo Montanari

The First European Revolution,
900–1200
R. I. Moore

Democracy in Europe
Maurice Agulhon

The European City

Leonardo Benevolo

Translated from the Italian by Carl Ipsen

BLACKWELL
Oxford UK & Cambridge USA

First published in 1993 by Blackwell Publishers and simultaneously by four other
publishers: © 1993 Beck, Munich (German); © 1993 Critica, Barcelona (Spanish);
© 1993 Editions du Seuil, Paris (French); © 1993 Laterza, Rome and Bari
(Italian).
Reprinted 1993

Blackwell Publishers
108 Cowley Road
Oxford OX4 1JF, UK

238 Main Street
Cambridge, Massachusetts 02142, USA

British Library Cataloguing in Publication Data
A CIP catalogue record for this book is available from the British Library.

Library of Congress Cataloging-in-Publication Data
Benevolo, Leonardo.
    The European city / Leonardo Benevolo : translated by Carl Ipsen.
        p.   cm. — (The Making of Europe)
    Includes bibliographical references and index.
    ISBN 0–631–17302–1
    1. Cities and towns — Europe — History.   2. Europe — Intellectual
life.
    I. Title.   II. Series.
    HT131.V46   1993
    307.76'094—dc20   92–34030
                                                                CIP

Typeset in 11 on 12½ pt Garamond by TecSet Ltd, Wallington, Surrey
Printed in Great Britain by T. J. Press (Padstow) Ltd, Cornwall

This book is printed on acid-free paper

To Paul Hofer

Contents

List of Illustrations

Series Editor's Preface

Europe is in the making. This is both a great challenge and one that can be met only by taking the past into account – a Europe without history would be orphaned and unhappy. Yesterday conditions today; today's actions will be felt tomorrow. The memory of the past should not paralyse the present: when based on understanding it can help us to forge new friendships, and guide us towards progress.

Europe is bordered by the Atlantic, Asia and Africa, its history and geography inextricably entwined, and its past comprehensible only within the context of the world at large. The territory retains the name given it by the ancient Greeks, and the roots of its heritage may be traced far into prehistory. It is on this foundation – rich and creative, united yet diverse – that Europe's future will be built.

The Making of Europe is the joint initiative of five publishers of different languages and nationalities: Beck in Munich; Blackwell in Oxford; Critica in Barcelona; Laterza in Rome; and le Seuil in Paris. Its aim is to describe the evolution of Europe, presenting the triumphs but not concealing the difficulties. In their efforts to achieve accord and unity the nations of Europe have faced discord, division and conflict. It is no purpose of this series to conceal these problems: those committed to the European enterprise will not succeed if their view of the future is unencumbered by an understanding of the past.

The title of the series is thus an active one: the time is yet to come when a synthetic history of Europe will be possible. The books we shall publish will be the work of leading historians, by no means all European. They will address crucial aspects of European history in every field – political, economic, social, religious and cultural. They will draw on that long historiographical tradition which stretches back to Herodotus, as well as on those conceptions and ideas which have transformed historical enquiry in the recent decades of the twentieth century. They will write readably for a wide public.

Our aim is to consider the key questions confronting those involved in Europe's making, and at the same time to satisfy the curiosity of the world at large: in short, who are the Europeans? where have they come from? whither are they bound?

Jacques Le Goff

Introduction

The European city came into being with Europe itself. In some sense it begot that region, historically defining European civilization and continuing to be its most salient characteristic as the subcontinent rose to world dominance. Today the European model still exercises a strong influence, whether positive or negative, on cities throughout the globe.

The history of the European city and the history of Europe are to a large extent one and the same, inextricable and well documented. So vast a topic cannot be made to fit inside one of the volumes of this series, which explore specific themes and moments of the European cultural heritage. Yet each of these volumes takes for granted the existence of the city, locus for the encounters and intersections of all historical processes. It is, however, possible to dedicate a single volume to the physical setting of the city. This setting has endured through time and constitutes today a unique means of communication between the present and the past, as well as a precondition imposed by the present on the future.

The nature of the city itself defines this function, and, paradoxically, checks its power for dynamic innovation. From the third millennium BC, the urban settlement has accelerated change by compressing spatial relations, and has given to human affairs the rapid pace that distinguishes history from prehistory. At the same time it has preserved an environment built in a particular historical epoch, passing it on to following epochs and linking to a degree the ways of life of each generation to the choices made by those preceding. It serves both as a motor pushing speedily ahead to the future and an anchor maintaining links to the past. In both cases it allows one to travel in time, jumping over a succession of events to approach distant places, moving either forward or back.

These observations still apply to the modern world. Improved communications make the effects of the physical concentration of human activity ever less significant, and so also the fact of living in the city rather than in the country; but the general physical setting in which we live maintains and increases its influence over our way of life, as mobility and the availability of free time increase.

The European city is an integral part of this setting, and the preservation of this material heritage is necessary if we are not to lose access to a collection of values not approachable by any other means: the identity of the places in which we live; the stable background against which the flow of diverse experiences that characterize each generation is given significance; the permanence of a 'centre' which changes more slowly than the periphery; a place where we can put together those common memories too weighty to be carried by each individual. As early as the middle of the nineteenth century, Baudelaire captured the dramatic difficulty of modern times:

> Le vieux Paris n'est plus (la forme d'une ville
> Change plus vite, hélas! que le coeur d'un mortel);
> . . .
> Paris change, mais rien dans ma mélancolie
> N'a bougé! palais neufs, échafaudages, blocs,
> Vieux faubourgs, tout pour moi devient allégorie,
> Et mes chers souvenirs sont plus lourds que des rocs.[1]

In the characters of this poetry – the swan escaped from its cage, Andromache led into exile by Pyrrhus, the *négresse amaigrie* who seeks the great palms of far-away Africa in the Parisian fog – we recognize not only the uprooted guests who inhabit our cities, but also the embarrassment of us all, made strangers by the physical destruction of the environment in which we have grown up.

The vital need to repair this break with the environment overwhelms other 'cultural' interests and creates the modern desire to preserve precisely those stone cityscapes built in the distant past. It is in these fragile settings, susceptible to the ravages of modern technology but preserved by that same technology, that the balance between individual and collective memory is for the moment maintained.

At the same time, the decisions we make today in response to our own contemporary problems regarding the systematization of the cities will be effective for many years, even when ways of thinking and of life will have changed; and as we engage in greater and more frequent transformations, we impinge to an ever greater extent on the lives of future generations, without being able adequately to predict and control the long-term effects of our actions. Believing ourselves capable of renewing at will the environment in which we live with the resources of modern technology, we have come to realize that the environments created are generally irreversible because of a series of interests and accomplished facts over which we have little control. These facts only increase the responsibility of the present age and make reflection on this aspect of European history especially pressing.

The sources needed for a general approach abound. The history of the urban organism is by its very nature a history of individual cases which must first be considered one at a time. Practically all the cities of Europe, large and small, have been studied in this way, often by the citizens themselves. A feeling of belonging has inspired both literary and scientific reconstruction of the material events that determine the urban visage.

The challenge lies in the comprehension of these many treatises, which might be collected in a computer but which by virtue of their complexity escape formalization and certainly exceed the limits of a single human brain. A city's physical form derives from a complex combination of geographical and historical factors; its various aspects constitute an array still more varied than that presented by those economic, social and cultural events, more easily traced to established conceptual categories.

The works of synthesis that exploit these sources are few and generally deal with the formation of the European city in the Middle Ages. Henri Pirenne's opinionated and controversial 1925 work[2] posed a challenge which has been taken up several times by following generations. Still rarer are studies of the 'Modern Era', during which both the modification of existing European cities and the transplanting of the European model in other parts of the world took place.

The more recent innovative phase, that of the Industrial Revolution, has been discussed primarily in functional terms and from a general perspective which has almost always failed to capture the historicity of the realization of mental models. The identification of the European city with the modern city throughout the globe has often been uncritically accepted, with the result that the important questions of its confrontation with other urban realities and of its hybrids both in Europe and in other continents are ignored.

Conventional modernity has taken the fact of the European city as an implicit given; yet even here the history of Europe defies easy classification. In order to comprehend fully the continuing dynamics of this history, we must recognize that ours is only one of the possible models for the modern city and so rethink within this modernity the specific shared and distinct aspects of the cities of Europe.

The attempt to describe even in general terms a universe of such diverse realities would require a book much larger than this one. The purpose of this series is to provide an up-to-date understanding of several specific aspects of the European cultural heritage, pushing the analysis only to the point required by this specificity. The paradox of such an undertaking is that multiplicity is one of the constituent characteristics of specificity. All that can be done is to present a selection of examples, grouped together into several significant historical periods, even though they do not represent a complete history of this continent. The Europe that interests us is not a geographical region but a historically determined reality. We must consider not simply those cities that exist within certain territorial boundaries, but those that emerged in the period when Europe acquired its distinctive identity and which accompanied its later development. From this point of view the periods of interest are:

> the emergence from the ancient world at the end of the tenth century (chapter 1);
> the formation of the medieval city, 1050–1350 (chapter 2);
> the period in which the city was brought to perfection, 1350–1500 (chapter 3);
> confrontation with the world, 1500–1600 (chapter 4);
> the difficult adaptation of the European city to the rules of perspective, 1600–1750 (chapter 5);
> the impact of industrialization, 1750–1890 (chapter 6);
> the transformation of the European city in the past hundred years (chapter 7).

Any discussion in this field requires the use of both text and images, and the selection of images poses great difficulties. They must present a small number of concrete settings which constitute a meaningful sequence without the aid of general discussion. The memory of those readers who live in or are familiar with the cities of Europe will, I hope, correct the inevitably arbitrary nature of the choices made for the illustrations in this volume.

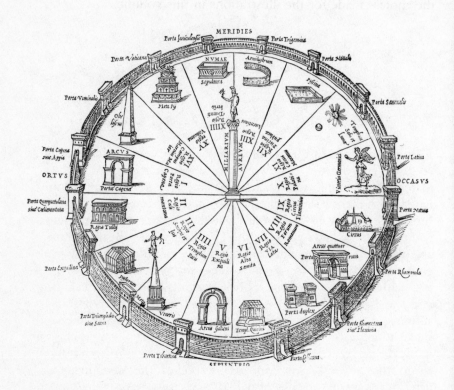

1 Schematic plan of Rome in the time of Augustus (engraving dated 1527).

1

Emergence from the Ancient World

The Idea of the City in the Classical Tradition

Europe was born of the dissolution of the ancient world; it would continue to confront that world from which it derived its basic material and intellectual structures. The city of antiquity dominated both institutional relationships and territorial organization. Indeed the crisis of the urban system was one of the principal components of the decline of the Classical world. Both literature and the collective imagination have long identified the city with civilization, passing on to us a series of occasionally awkward associations between those words deriving from the Greek *polis* and the Latin *urbs* and *civitas*. The fall of the imperial state is summed up in the destruction of the eponymous city, Rome; and the disintegration of organized society finds its physical expression in the destruction of the urban landscape. Visiting northern Italy in about the year 387, St Ambrose wrote of the 'semidirutarum urbium cadavera' (corpses of half-ruined cities).[1] After the sack of Rome in 410, St Augustine preserved the idea of the city in the supernatural world and described the Christian religious order as the City of God, to be compared to the city of man which perishes under the weight of its own sins.[2]

It will be useful to recall briefly the combination of cultural and institutional motivations included in this concept at the end of the ancient period. The city came into existence in the third and second millennia BC in Mesopotamia and in the valleys of the Nile, Indus and Yellow River as a centre of command for the accumulation and exchange of the excess agricultural production of the more fertile areas. The novelty of this event, which separates myth from history, is clearly recorded in the first written texts: at the head of the oldest Sumerian royal list (from the late third millennium), one reads: 'As soon as the heavenly reign came to the earth, it flourished in Eridu.'[3] The boundary between city and country, the line that divides the world into two distinct parts, long dominated the physical setting as well as mental and institutional organization. The city is an enclosure, or a series of enclosures, in which the art of manipulating medium and short distances – that which from then on would be described as 'architecture' – reached maturity, while the older art, which aimed at the occupation and modification of the unlimited landscape, was gradually forgotten. The pyramids that emerge from the constructed landscape of Egypt and Mesopotamia and are visible from great distances as part of the natural landscape mark for a certain period the transition between these two approaches. Within the city, the house, palace and temple are each partial enclosures which gain importance according to their degree of segregation. One need only recall the common structure of the temple and of entombment in Egypt, both characterized by multiple protective layers to ward off a hostile and feared outside world.

Greek civilization reinvented the city as a collective horizon, worthy of man for its completeness and requiring both a balanced external relation with the countryside and a calculated and controlled internal measure. This theoretical idea is expressed by Aristotle in the following well-known passage:

> If all communities aim at some good, the state or political community, which is the highest of all, and which embraces all the rest, aims at a good in a greater degree than any other, and at the highest good . . . In the first place there must be a union of those who cannot exist without each other; namely, of male and female, that the race may continue . . . and of natural ruler and subject, that both may be preserved . . . Out of these two relationships the first thing to arise is the family . . . But when several families are united, and the association aims at something more than the supply of daily needs, the first society to be formed is the village . . . When several villages are united in a single complete community, large enough to be nearly or quite self-sufficing, the state comes into existence, originating in the bare needs of life, and

continuing in existence for the sake of a good life. And therefore, if the earlier forms of society are natural, so is the state, for it is the end of them, and the nature of a thing is its end. For what each thing is when fully developed, we call its nature . . . Hence it is evident that the state is a creation of nature, and that man is by nature a political animal . . . Now, that man is more of a political animal than bees or any other gregarious animals is evident. Nature, as we often say, makes nothing in vain, and man is the only animal who has the gift of speech. And whereas mere voice is but an indication of pleasure or pain, and is therefore found in other animals . . . the power of speech is intended to set forth the expedient and inexpedient, and therefore likewise the just and the unjust. And it is a characteristic of man that he alone has any sense of good and evil, of just and unjust, and the like, and the association of living beings who have this sense makes a family and a state. Further, the state is by nature clearly prior to the family and to the individual . . . The proof that the state is a creation of nature and prior to the individual is that the individual, when isolated, is not self-sufficing; and therefore he is like a part in relation to the whole. But he who is unable to live in society, or who has no need because he is sufficient for himself, must be either a beast or a god.[4]

As has often been noted, the Greek city was an 'open city', and legally included the rural population which, when necessary, found protection within its walls. It presented a single landscape made up of parts which, though of differing function and importance, were none the less of a similar visual and metric scale. Public, as opposed to private, buildings and spaces predominated and gave to the urban setting that perfect and refined character called for by the Aristotelian definition. The columned porticoes that surround the temples and monumental buildings accomplished a gradual transition from internal space to the external and public; architecture gave shape and uniform dignity to the entire human environment.

In terms of their universal justification, this idea and this spatial model survived even in those states that far exceeded the Aristotelian *myrioi*, or population of ten thousand, the upper limit for a functioning democratic assembly. The Roman Empire was in a sense the legal extension of the *urbs*, and functioned as 'a confede-

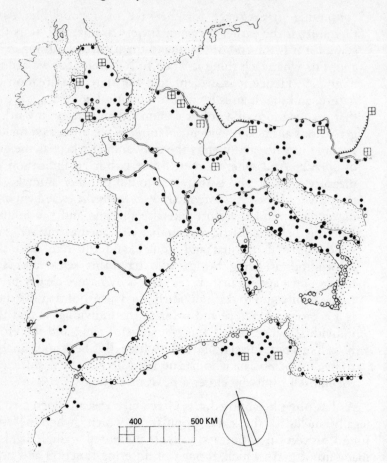

2   *Cities of the Roman Empire.*

ration of urban cells, held together by a skeleton provincial administration, but fully autonomous in internal affairs.'[5] The empire joined together a large number of Mediterranean city-states and created others where they previously did not exist. It established on the shores of the Mediterranean Sea a continuous network of several thousand cities, both large and small, walled and unwalled, and frequently conforming to a unified geometric

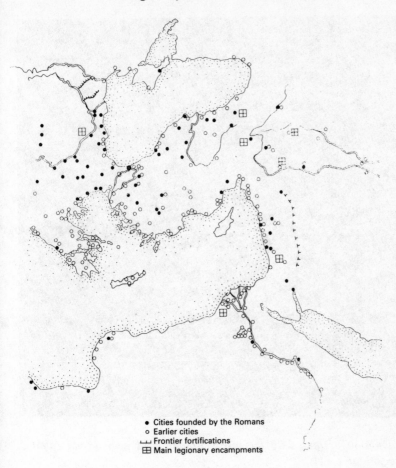

• Cities founded by the Romans
○ Earlier cities
⊔⊔ Frontier fortifications
⊞ Main legionary encampments

design that ordered the various public and private architectural elements. Within the enduring and peaceful setting of the Roman Empire, this rational design flowed from the cities to the hinterland and ordered the countryside according to the regular forms of agricultural plots, roads, bridges, aqueducts, borders, canals and ports: the functional supports and omnipresent image of a homogeneous civilization spread over a vast geographic area.

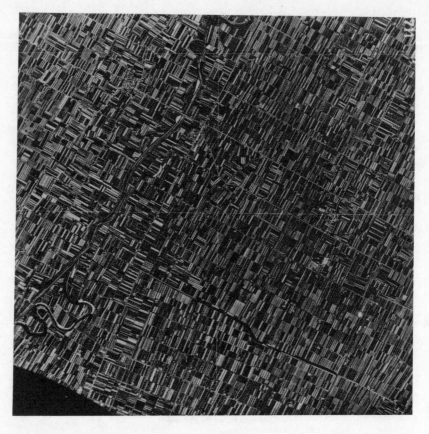

3 *Division of land into lots on a Roman grid near Imola (photo: Anderson, no. 281).*

Urban Transformations of the Late Empire

Beginning in the third century AD – with the barbarian invasions and the weakening of the imperial state – the security of the cities declined, while they acquired still greater importance as fortified centres for the protection of endangered civil institutions.

Cities that had grown freely, protected by the *pax Romana* and their distance from foreign borders, were forced to surround themselves with walls and so choose a definite perimeter to consolidate and defend. This task almost always required the contraction of a large and discontinuous urban centre and the incorporation of natural obstacles (rivers, irregular terrain), the original pre-Roman walls (in the Etruscan cities of central Italy – Volterra, Perugia – and in the oldest colonial cities), and the great structures arranged around the urban centres – the Roman *circus* (Milan), the amphitheatre (Périgueux, Tours, Florence, Lucca) and the aqueduct (Nîmes).

In Rome itself the ring of the Aurelian walls was built in AD 274 and surrounded an area of 1,350 hectares, only a fraction of the immense inhabited area filling the plain on either side of the Tiber. It incorporated the Castra Praetoria, the Castrense amphitheatre and several lengths of aqueduct. In Gaul the fortified cities often incorporated only a fraction of the previously open cities: in Bordeaux a quarter, in Nîmes a seventh, in Autun a twentieth. The regional capitals of the Tetrarchs – Trevirorum (Trier), Mediolanum (Milan), Sirmium (Sirmione), and Nicomedia – were chosen for their strategic location near border rivers – the Rhine, the Danube – or areas of military operation, and were equipped with fortifications appropriate to their functions, though at times, as in Trier, these became too extensive when their importance declined. Some of the most important walled cities from this period – Dijon, Bourges, Poitiers, Mainz – continued to function and accommodate urban development into the late Middle Ages.

In 326 Constantinople was designated the new capital of the empire because of the exceptional defensive possibilities offered by its geographical setting. Enormous lines of fortification were built by Constantine (330) and Theodosius (414) which enclosed an area of 1,400 hectares, about the size of Rome. Water arrived by way of underground aqueducts, which could not be cut off by enemies, and was then stored in vast cisterns. Distinguished both by its advantageous location and the truly imperial scale of the technical undertaking, Constantinople long served as the model of the walled city: unassailable, dominating a vast land- and seascape, and possessing a natural port – the Golden Horn – which could be blocked by a chain drawn across the mouth of the Bosporus. Throughout the Middle Ages, Constantinople dominated the collective imagination of both East and West, seat of the successors to the Caesars and source of the most refined works of art and craft in the whole of the Mediterranean basin. Here, too, in a supreme

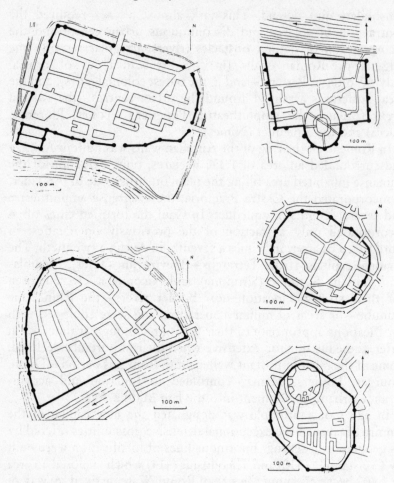

4   *Late imperial city fortifications in Roman Gaul: Rouen, Chalon-sur-Saône, Tours, Senlis, Périgueux.*

effort at conservation, were kept the greatest treasures of the Graeco-Roman world – the sculptures of Phidias, the paintings of Zeuxis and Parrhasius, the tripod from Delphi.

Following the division of the empire at the death of Theodosius, the capital of the Western Empire was transferred to Ravenna, a city defended by the surrounding marshes, but connected to the sea, and so the empire, by way of the Augustan port excavated in the Classe area. The original Roman *oppidum* was repeatedly

5   *Constantinople as imagined in the West in the fifteenth century (from Schedel,* Cronaca, Nuremberg, 1493).

enlarged in the fifth century and enriched with both civil and religious monuments which stood as models of court architecture for all the West.

Beginning in the fourth century, the symbols and buildings of the Christian religion came to characterize and transform to some degree the urban organism. Most Christian churches were linked to the burial of saints and to cemeteries which, according to Roman law, had to be located outside the city walls. In Rome the majority of the Constantine basilicas – St Peter's, San Paolo, San Lorenzo, Sant'Agnese, Santi Marcellino e Pietro, and San Sebastiano – are all outside the Aurelian wall, while two others – San Giovanni in Laterano and Santa Croce in Gerusalemme – are only

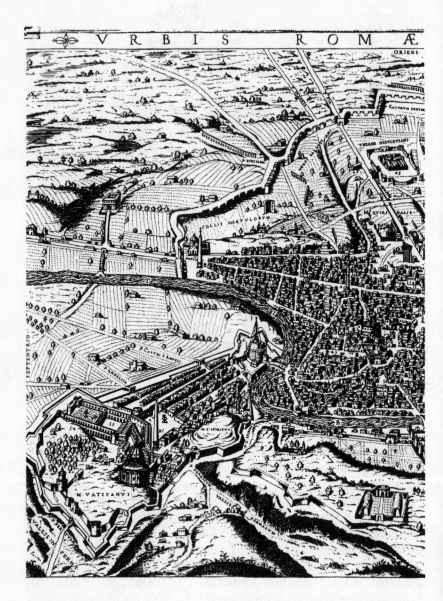

6 *Papal Rome.*

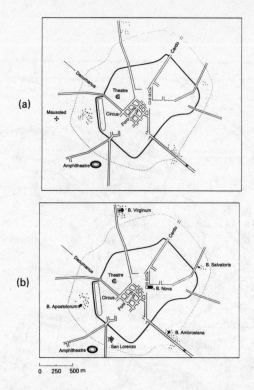

7a and b Maps of Milan c. 300 and 400 AD (from R. Krautheimer,
Three Christian Capitals. Topography and Politics, *Berkeley: University*
of California Press, 1983).

just inside it. The cross of churches formed by St Peter's, San Paolo,
San Giovanni and Santa Maria Maggiore was completed around the
year 365; they all stand outside the legal limit of the Servian wall
and are centred on the Colosseum, permanent symbol of the city.
This arrangement became one of the principal elements of urban
organization and defined the polycentric character of the papal city
from that date forward.

In Milan, St Ambrose created not only the Santa Tecla cathedral
in the centre of the city, but also several basilicas outside the walls:
that which carries his name (later replaced by the famous Romanesque church), San Simpliciano, San Nazaro and San Lorenzo.
The 'four crosses' built outside the walls of Bologna may have been

constructed following his instructions. The great imperial churches of Constantinople – St Irene and St Sophia, connected to the palace at the peak of the promontory, and the sepulchral Church of the Sacred Apostles – are the reference points which charted the city's development and dominated the urban setting even before their reconstruction under Justinian.

These buildings reveal not only the monumental scale of Roman public works, but also a break with the Classical architectural tradition which had an important impact on the urban scale. The fourth century witnessed an attempt to create large vaulted spaces in conformity with Classical tradition, which is to say tying the form of these spaces to a framework of normalized sculptural elements hierarchically arranged – the Graeco-Roman architectural method – which would permit the subject to take in the entire environment with a single glance before passing through it. The vaulted basilica of Maxentius in the Roman Forum is one of the most important examples in this regard. A different constructive and formal model was chosen for the churches of this period, that of the flat-roofed basilica. Less expensive, less enduring and statically less of a challenge, it was a model in which columns, trabeations and arches became secondary elements, perhaps much in evidence from a decorative point of view, but not tied to the proportions of the rooms. The size of the space could not be judged in advance, but was apprehended as the subject made his way through a continuity of like objects.

These objects make up the well-known panoply of traditional visual elements which create the sumptuous environments described in the texts of the period: the inscription on the golden cross given by Helena and Constantine in St Peter's reads 'fulgore coruscans aula' (a hall gleaming with splendour). Yet this development also initiated the disintegration of the ancient architectural world, every element of which could be rethought in its own right. And from this rethinking a new buildingscape emerged.

The Crisis of the Cities after the Fall of the Western Empire

The reorganization described above remained viable in the East for ten centuries; in the West, however, it was thrown into disarray after the fifth century by the fall of the imperial state. The late

Classical urban settings rapidly became oversized and not fully exploited by the populations that continued to inhabit them.

The crisis of the urban system must be understood in the larger context of the changes that altered the course of history in much of the world. From the third to the fifth century, the 'barbarian' migrations shook the entire Eurasian continent, for reasons which are still not entirely clear. The parallel between the fall of the Roman Empire and that of the Han Empire in China has been noted many times, each accompanied by the spread of an interior and 'foreign' religion, respectively Christianity and Buddhism.

This parallelism breaks down in the sixth century. Reunification, achieved after 581 by the Suy and the Tang Dynasties, enabled Classical Chinese civilization to survive, reinforced by the ethical character of the imperial tradition, the uniformity of the written (as opposed to the spoken) language, a large population and the practice of intensive agriculture. The new capital, Chang-an, measured about 7,500 hectares within a rectangle of walls and more than 20,000 within an enclosed park (including the remains of the previous Han city), dimensions unmatched in the pre-industrial world. Scientific, technological, economic and administrative achievements made Chinese society indisputably the most advanced until the encounter with European expansion in the nineteenth century.

Justinian did not enjoy similar success. From the seventh century, the Byzantine Empire coexisted with the Arab Caliphate. These two contrasting worlds remained for many centuries the principal civilized and urbanized areas of western Eurasia. They included several important cities with a population of many hundreds of thousands: Constantinople (the last ancient capital enclosed within its walls) as well as Baghdad, Cordoba and Palermo, three extensive city-oases employing the Persian methods of irrigated cultivation. Western Christendom remained on the periphery, incomparably poorer and politically divided. Neither Theodoric nor Charlemagne nor the Ottos succeeded in reunifying this smaller area. Technical, economic and administrative conditions did not meet the requirements of a large city – Rome or the Tetrarch capitals of Trier or Milan – and only in a few cases did several tens of thousands of inhabitants remain within the city walls.

Yet it was just this backwardness and lack of unity which cleared the way for a vast, open-minded and ingenious experiment, an experiment that would form the basis of a new civilization, both materially and philosophically. During the 'dark' ages from the seventh to the tenth centuries, a period of a dozen generations, Western Christianity was radically transformed, and a new historical reality emerged from the traditional geography of the Mediterranean world, a reality which would henceforth be called Europe.

The central problem for the already urbanized areas was to maintain and adapt the existing Classical legacy; the great infrastructures together with the buildings that previously filled public functions – baths, theatres, amphitheatres, circuses and warehouses – had been dismantled. The longevity of the physical setting relative to other elements of civil life created the anachronism of a society occupying the shell of a previous civilization with which it could compete neither technically nor intellectually. Coexistence with the 'ruins' of the ancient world would remain a constant of European civilization and transmitted – in addition to highly perfected architectural forms, still models centuries later – the physical sense of another, ever-present civilization, both foreign and familiar at the same time. It also inspired a series of general reflections on the fragility of human works and on those greater forces – the ravages of time, the fickleness of fortune – which have long accompanied both the individual and collective European sentiment.

The decay of this immense architectural heritage occurred gradually. The structural organism of Rome survived in large part until the Norman invasion of 1085, though the water supply via the eastern aqueducts and the food supply via Ostia and the riverside warehouses became problematic after the first invasions and ceased entirely during the Gothic War between 535 and 553. The surviving population was concentrated in the low areas on either side of the river, and this singular high-water bed gradually became the new Rome, while the useless ruins of the great ancient buildings dominated the surrounding hills as far as the distant Aurelian walls. The monumental centre itself, the forum, lay on the outskirts of the papal city, and would remain so until the second half of the nineteenth century. Distinguished both by its

8 *Rome: the Colosseum still surrounded by open country in the early twentieth century (photo: Anderson, no. 281).*

past prestige and the presence of the Holy See, Rome was also symbolic in its ruined state, and already the prototype of the imperfect city which would characterize the subsequent history of Europe.

The Colosseum remained a dominating element of the Roman setting. Intended by the Flavian emperors to celebrate the public reappropriation of Nero's immense private sanctuary, it had from its creation occupied a central and unusual position. When no longer functional, it acquired an ambiguous and mysterious significance: a compendium of the lost pagan city, scene of early Christian martyrdom, and 'temple of demons'.[6] Its seeming indestructibility somehow links it to the survival of Rome in the present and the future.

The histories of other cities differed greatly because of a variety of military, economic and cultural factors. In Italy, Spain, southern Gaul and the Rhineland, municipalities continued to function, some until the end of the eighth century, preserving more or less an urban organism. Theodoric split his residence between Ravenna and Pavia, after which the latter city became the definitive capital for the Ostrogothic kings who restored the baths and the amphitheatre. Equipped with a sturdy wall after the Frankish attack of 260, Barcelona became a royal residence in the fifth century under Ataulphus and Placidia; it prospered during the Visigoth renaissance of the seventh century, subsequently interrupted by Arab invasion. Of the Merovingian kings, Clovis made his home in Paris, and Childeric had the arenas of Paris and Soissons restored. The Lombard kings remained in Pavia and expanded the city to the east while building a new royal palace. Other cities atrophied. Ravenna remained under the rule of Constantinople until the Lombard conquest of 751 and gradually declined to provincial status: the port silted up; the area within the too large circle of walls was largely uninhabited, and the great monuments, symbols of imperial authority, were stripped by the Lombards, the Franks and the Venetians. In the following centuries, marble from Ravenna appeared in European cities aspiring to greatness as far away as Aachen. The 'Sun King', an equestrian statue of a Roman emperor, was taken to Pavia, only to be melted down by the Jacobins in 1796. Other cities that lost their previous political and economic role suffered a similar fate: Bologna, which shrank from 70 to 25 hectares; Trier, where only a few clusters of population remained within the vast late imperial enclosure, insufficient to impede the ruinous Norman invasion of 882; and the cities of southern Italy, which continued their existence under the Byzantine Empire only with difficulty. Others disappeared entirely, like Salona, destroyed by the Avars in 614, and most of the African cities following the Arab advance of the seventh century.

At the same time, while the Germanic peoples under the Carolingian and Merovingian kings settled in the northern plains, on the confines and outside what had been the Roman Empire, a network of military and commercial centres was established in these regions as well, expanding the urbanized area of the continent. These centres included the trading posts along the lower Rhine and the North Sea (Quentovic, Duurstede), the Scandinavian *wike* (Birka, Haithabu), the Saxon and Frankish castles between the Rhine and the Elbe, the important fortified and commercial settlements of Moravia (like Mikulkice) and of Bohemia (like Prague), the English towns founded by the Anglo-Saxon kings, and the *poblaciones* which accompanied the reconquest of Arab territories in Spain begun in 718. The presence of ecclesiastical sees in each of these geographical regions testified to common religious allegiance and long remained the only specifically urban centres of power, giving the new settlements the potential character of a city.

The decline of the Roman urban setting and nascent urbanization in the areas that had remained outside Roman influence served gradually to bring the continental extremes, from the Mediterranean to the North Sea, into a sort of urban equality. At the same time, many regional and local differences emerged upon which large-scale political organizations had only limited and weak influence. In Italy, southern France, Spain, and Africa prior to the Arab invasion, the Roman city survived more or less intact; in a second area, which extended to the Rhine, the Germanic frontier and the Danube, the more remote Roman cities remained islands in a rural sea; while in a third, unbordered, area, a new system of isolated strongholds was taking root. A new unity, made up of differences, emerged and would for ever remain a characteristic of Europe.

The Emerging Characteristics of the Western Urban System

The peculiarities of this situation revealed the first outlines of the European city to come, both in the ways in which the inherited centres were modified and reused and in the logic that guided the new settlements.

In the first place, the idea of the city lost its general and systematic connotations, while acquiring a new and radical adherence to its geographical and natural setting. Each pre-existing city was mentally assimilated to the territory that it occupied, territory which human inventiveness would begin to exploit from scratch. When the small fortified Cité, an island of 8 hectares in the Seine, became inadequate for the revival of urban life in Paris, further expansion took place not on the left bank site of the Roman city, but instead on a semicircular area on the right bank bounded by the swamps of a prehistoric river. This area previously had been used by the Gallic tribes as a place of worship and assembly. As

Edith Ennen has observed, the Germans understood the Roman cities in terms of their idea of castle (*Burg*), adopting the name Augsburg rather than Augusta, and Kolnaburg rather than Colonia.[7] Traces and memories of pre-Roman settlements re-emerged in the landscape as in language: Celtic, Illyrian, Punic. In Rome, the accumulated ruins of ancient buildings became artificial 'hills' – Monte Savello, Monte Giordano, and so on – which have from that time become part of the urban topography, additions to the natural hills of Rome.

In the second place, the distribution of urban architectural and symbolic weight changed together with the balance between the different parts. We have already referred to the peripheral placement of the first Christian churches, often arranged in a cross along the main transport arteries. Evidence of other 'crosses of churches' exists for Lyon and Reims, and subsequently for many medieval cities. The location of an important sanctuary outside the urban area occasionally resulted in a shift of the centre: in Bonn, the sepulchral church of St Cassius, situated outside the *castrum*, became the cathedral and, already by the ninth century, constituted the new centre of the city. In Italy the difficult blending of the local populations with the Lombards led the conquerors to establish appendage settlements: Pavia has already been mentioned; in Bologna they established their own religious centre of Santo Stefano outside Porta Ravegnana; and in Benevento around Santa Sofia. The coexistence of different Christian confessions, as in Ravenna under the Goths, created distinct religious centres and associated quarters of the city.

Meanwhile, the internal urban framework underwent profound transformations. In both the large and small Roman cities, the inward-facing sections of the blocks lost much of their original function – as individual or collective residences and public buildings – and were split up by new crooked streets which allowed their use as workshops and smaller residences. Some of the more conspicuous structures – temples, theatres, amphitheatres, circuses, aqueducts, and now useless reservoirs – served as fortified strongholds. Occasionally a single great structure – the royal palace of Diocletian in Spalato (Split) – would encompass an entire city.

Free from the constraints of an existing form, the new settlements were designed independently of Classical models. Instead,

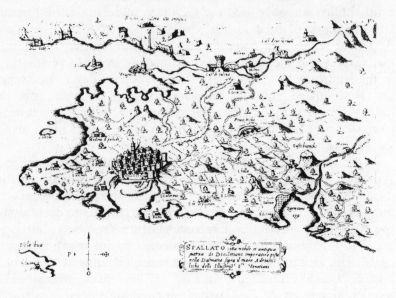

9　*Split (Spalato), with the town built inside Diocletian's palace walls (seventeenth-century engraving).*

they conformed to the necessities of defence and commerce, for which the architectural heritage of Rome was poorly suited, serving only an emblematic purpose, to dignify religious and municipal centres or to symbolize membership in that cultural universe.

The landscape in which these two types of settlement were situated, and which served to distance them from one another, was a space expanded by the new relationship with the northern areas and by the slow and risky nature of communications; it was a space in which human traces were often difficult to find or to decipher. Whatever the type, cities were above all places of precarious refuge from the dangers of this indefinite space in which the territorial organization of the Roman state had been lost and a new organization only just begun. Outside the city gates one immediately encountered forests, swamps, uninhabited countryside and mountains, areas which, according to the Christian conception of the world, had lost their pagan sacredness and belonged to a created universe (though one always potentially open to human initiative).

The range of technical and mental intervention in the environment was drastically diminished. Those who lived in this setting became accustomed to viewing it from close to while not possessing the means for its representation or for its large-scale control. Architecture lost its vastness, and the individual elements – columns and sculpted decorations, removed from pagan buildings and incorporated into Christian ones – were each admired for their own workmanship, while the regularity of the whole was irrevocably lost.

The new structures built in the West long depended on ancient and eastern prototypes and often revealed a longing for identity with a distant, and more advanced, world; the Palatine Chapel of Charlemagne in Aachen is an example, based on models from Ravenna. The search for a compositional whole, which constituted the driving force of Byzantine architecture, was abandoned. Volumetric elements were flattened against the walls so that, within the restricted spaces allowed by smaller and more contained cities, they could be seen from close to as chiaroscuro embellishments on the stonemasonry.

The inability to manage large-scale structures – roads, bridges, aqueducts, reservoirs, ports – resulted in their no longer being counted among the products of human industry, and the surviving ancient structures of this category were likened to the natural landscape or ascribed to some mysterious manifestation of supernatural powers. Great engineering feats – which Frontinus in the first century AD compared to the useless 'marvels' of the Hellenistic world and characterized as products of an architecturally superior civilization based on rationality and public utility – became 'bridges of the devil' in the collective imagination, created to challenge man and his heavenly protectors.

It was life's new setting, emerging in the Middle Ages from among the ruins of a vanished world, that would count for the future. Conceptual measurements were restricted, but formed a homogeneous system in which the distinguishing characteristics of the classical city lost importance. The urban residences of the barbarian kings – in Ravenna, Verona, Pavia, Bordeaux, Toulouse, Barcelona, Toledo, Aachen and Worms – were enclosed courts, copies of ancient palaces; occasionally they actually took over the latter, like the governor's palace in Cologne which became the palace of the Merovingian kings. Limited technological and organizational resources enforced dependency in many ways upon the surrounding environment. For purposes of worship, churches required close communication between internal and external spaces. For these various reasons, all the individual spaces of the city tended to combine into one continuous space. Highly stylized masonry impinged upon the smaller open spaces, and architectural detail, rather than characterize a building in its own right, became a tool for presenting a building to the public space. Little by little, the inward facing walls turned outward, and a unitary and multiform urban environment emerged, characterized by the sequence of these new structural organisms. The degradation of ancient structures and their integration into a new geographical system which opened to the north were the key points of a qualitative change that announced the new setting of the coming centuries.

2

The Creation of a New Urban System

The last, feared invaders of Western Christianity – Arabs, Scandinavians and Hungarians – were either contained or else settled down after the mid-tenth century. Subsequently, the western edge of Eurasia was free from outside threats of the sort that continued to trouble the Byzantine Empire, the Arab world and the Chinese Empire.

The Europe that emerged already possessed the new techniques of cultivation (triennial rotation, the use of draught animals made possible by new harnessing methods, and the combining of agriculture and the raising of livestock) which allowed for the exploitation of both level and hilly land, as well as new sources of energy (water- and windmills) and the nautical instruments perfected in the northern seas. The combination of relative peace, generally mild climatic conditions and the availability of new cultivable territory both within Europe and without led to the initiation of a cycle of demographic and productive increase which continued until the mid-fourteenth century.

As part of this process, cities became specialized centres of secondary and tertiary activities and were not subjugated to a central political authority, as they were in China or the ancient world. Each city, whether the complement of a small agricultural hinterland or completely independent like Venice, engaged in a wide range of commercial, industrial, financial and cultural initiatives, while competing with each other on both a continental and a global scale.

The existence of many differentiated centres was a decisive factor in speeding the spread of this development. From the eleventh century, the cities acquired autonomy in a number of ways and held their own against weak and distant state powers. This appropriation of responsibility – lacking in the Arab and oriental worlds – is the source of the distinctive vital character of European cities, and helped to define European civilization and contribute to its global success.

The enormous variety and originality of the urban settings designed and created between the eleventh and fourteenth centuries derives from this situation. Lacking the resources of a large territory, medieval cities were of limited size, considerably smaller than the ancient, Muslim or oriental capitals. Yet their design was of a character which suited them even when they became larger, and which, living in them today, we continue to admire. They are small settings of global scope, centres of diverse and competing economic and cultural worlds; and they are testimony to the possibility of reducing the world to a domestic scale.

This variety cannot be contained in a single description, nor in a classification by types which do not relate to models present in the culture of the period. One can, however, attempt to explain the mechanisms by which the array of concrete examples came to be, and choose several examples to describe in their uniqueness.

The Italian Maritime Cities

In the ninth and tenth centuries, trade with the East was so limited as to be centred primarily on the small city of Amalfi, a fortified landing on a steep, mountainous coast which an Arab traveller in 977 called 'the wealthiest, noblest and most famous city of Lombardy'.[1] While Amalfi maintained colonies throughout the Mediterranean, the great ports of antiquity – Ostia, Pozzuoli, Brindisi – languished in disuse. The victory of Otto I over the Hungarians (955), the Byzantine reconquest of Crete (960) and the expulsion of the Saracens from their base in Frassineto (973) opened new areas to trade. These developments benefited primarily Venice – which began to expand into the Adriatic and the eastern Mediterranean – and the cities of the upper Tyrrhenian – Pisa and Genoa – which took control of Corsica and Sardinia at the beginning of the eleventh century. Amalfi was overthrown at the end of the eleventh century by the Normans and

10 *Amalfi: aerial view (photo: Fotocielo, no. 1/231).*

their Pisan allies. Subsequently, Venice, Pisa and Genoa grew rapidly. During the twelfth century, each acquired its shape and fully displayed its own originality, consciously aiming to challenge both the heritage of antiquity and the vast Mediterranean world.

It was Venice above all that emerged as a mercantile city-state on the edge of the Western political world, immune from the continental feudal system. In the *Chronologia magna ab origine mundi ad annum millesimum tergentesimum quadragesimum sextum* (Great Chronology from the Beginning of the World to the year 1346), there appears a fourteenth-century map of Venice, a realistic representation, completely different from the symbolic images

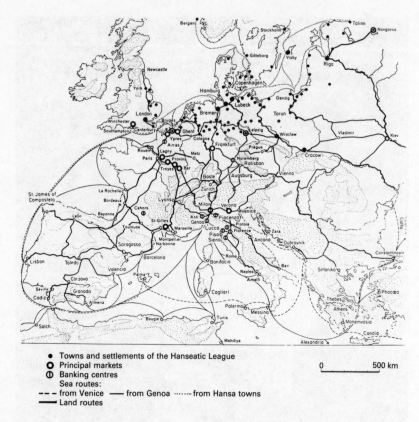

11 European communications, eleventh to thirteenth century (from R. Lopez, The Birth of Europe, London: Dent, 1966).

which accompanied the descriptions of cities to the end of the fifteenth century. The shape of the city derives directly from its actual geographical setting, which is not the uniform mirror of water which presents itself to the viewer, but includes the complex and invisible underwater terrain. Using a darker colour, the map distinguishes within the uniform background of the lagoon a network of navigable canals. The urban organism, a compact weft of built-up islands and parishes, is logically placed at the confluence of the Grand Canal and the Giudecca Canal, not far from their common mouth on the open sea. This was a conscious choice which suppressed nature in order to create a city, artificially fixing

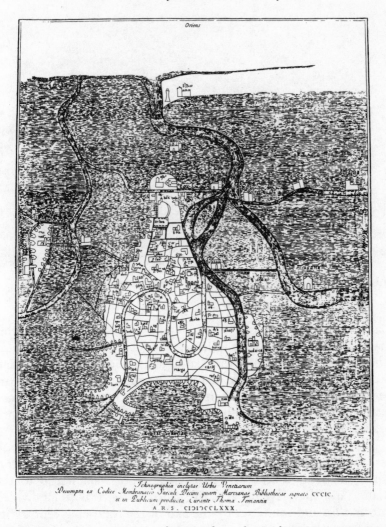

12 *Fourteenth-century map of Venice from the Codex Marcianus (repro-duced in an engraving dated 1780).*

the changing outlines of the canals and assigning a convenient limit to the built-up area. The well-known dolphin-shaped perimeter intersects the waterways at the desired points, where the work of land reclamation was intentionally halted. The area of construction is large enough to be filled by the pronounced S of the Grand

13   *Venice: waterfront of the San Marco complex (photo: Benevolo).*

Canal – but in such a way that no point is too distant from this major artery – and extends to the east to include the Arsenal dock. The commercial centre of the Rialto, halfway along the canal, and the political centre of San Marco at its mouth are not far apart because of the Canal's sharp bend, and establish the minor diametrical axis without interrupting the communication network branching throughout the entire city.

The design and construction of this splendid organism took place almost entirely in the period between the ninth century, when the Doge's seat was transferred from Malamocco to the Rialto, and the eleventh century, when the city was subdivided into *confini* and *contrade*; by the end of the following century its monumental definition was virtually complete. San Marco was rebuilt between 1060 and 1094, following the model of the Church of the Holy Apostles in Constantinople. The Doge's fortress was transformed around 1175 with the opening of the L-shaped piazza in front of the church, on to which the loggias of the palace faced; this was the scene of the meeting between Frederick I and Pope Alexander III in 1177. Venice became the equal of Constantinople and, after the conquest of 1204, took on the role of heir to the Eastern capital. Some of the most exclusive characteristics of the city derived from this direct link, which placed Venice beyond the stylistic border between east and west and isolated it from the rest of Italy, including Ravenna. Out of this extraordinary hybridization came, above all, the system of aligned walls, solid at ground level and joined together above by mullioned façades. Previously used in Constantinople with a completely different relationship to external space, in Venice this system consisted of the continuous walls lining the canals. The Venetian façades took on successively Romanesque, Gothic, Renaissance and Baroque forms without losing their original function of throwing open the internal environments to the outside.

Geographical security, political stability and the efficiency of the collective government made surrounding walls and the fortification of individual buildings unnecessary, which in turn allowed for a close correlation between the finishing of public and private spaces along a screen of façades, filtering images in both directions. The rigorous uniformity of elevation imposed by the water's surface, rhythmically pulsing with the tides, dictated the entire deployment of the city and its double set of paths and canals, crossing each other with the minimum common sacrifice (the pedestrian climbing over the bridge, the boatman ducking under it). Out of this fabric, defined by the horizontal surface of the water, the bell towers of the churches emerge and signal from a distance the greater and lesser parts of the city. The golden spire of the campanile of San Marco, the most important of all, could be seen by sailors from a distance of 200 stades, about 40 km.[2]

The very life of the city depended upon the lagoon's intermediate character, somewhere between sea and *terra firma*, which had originally formed it. To preserve this character the engineers of the Republic eventually undertook considerable projects: the mouths of the Brenta and Piave rivers, which emptied into the lagoon, were altered to prevent silting; new canals were dug to facilitate the passage of ships and ensure water circulation; the sand bars of the several Lidos between the lagoon and the sea were reinforced to protect against storms. In addition, severe laws were passed to protect the environment.

Both the political and the physical construction of the lagoon city – object of mythical admiration throughout the West, entirely unique and 'founded on the impossible'[3] – depended on the same tension, a mixture of reason and fear. It was the only European city-state to compete successfully with the national states of the sixteenth century, and it remained a world power until the eighteenth, governed by a constitution that was unchanged from the Serrata del Maggior Consiglio (1297) until the Treaty of Campo Formio (1797). Venice was slow to feel the impact of world classicism, and did so according to broad oscillations. In return, it offered a new visual civilization, given expression by the painters of the sixteenth century and by Palladio, and spread throughout the world in the following centuries.

Loss of political autonomy threatened the coherence and, down to the present day, the physical survival of the city. The particularism of Venice cannot withstand the test of integration with the outside world; and it may be that even the interest which the entire world takes in this unique city will not be enough to save it.

Unlike Venice, Pisa, located on the lagoon at the mouth of the Arno river, was inhabited from Etruscan and Roman times. It became important when Augustus established a port on the southern edge of the Sinus Pisanus. In the Middle Ages, Pisa used the still functioning port and was already important in the epochs of Charlemagne and the Ottos. Although tracing to a degree the ancient settlement, it was essentially a new city, conforming approximately to the Classical grid but adapted to the curve of the river and the changing level of the terrain.

The main development of Pisa took place between the beginning of the eleventh century, when the municipal government was established, and the second half of the twelfth, when at the height of its prosperity the surrounding city walls were built (enclosing 114 hectares). These would continue to define the city, and were even too large after the political crisis of the thirteenth century.

The coherence of the urban form is based, as in Venice, on a remarkable continuity of construction, and so on the homogeneity of a building fabric consisting of equal modules rhythmically repeated both in civil building and in the large religious monuments. The attached tower-houses with their vertical cornerstones and low brick arches are grouped together after the Roman technique for large utilitarian structures (bridges, aqueducts, amphitheatres) and so freed from an overall geometric form; they themselves become the generating elements of an open composition. The rows of columns and arches in the churches constitute solemn organisms following palaeochristian models. The always

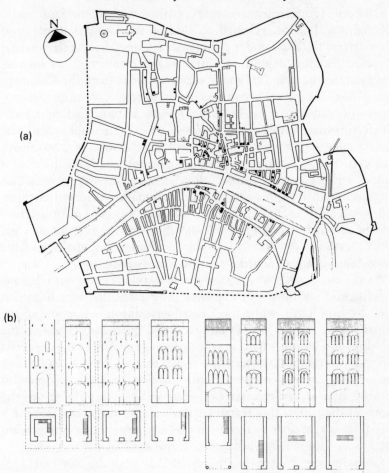

14   *Map of medieval Pisa with diagrams of the surviving tower-houses
(from G. Fanelli and F. Trivisonno,* Città antica in Toscana, *Florence:
Sansoni, 1982).*

incomplete and repeatable nature of the initial layout allows for
extensions, interruptions and other unexpected developments in
the same structure, as well as the introduction into the composition
of other heterogeneous motifs taken from all regions of the
Mediterranean.

The operation described above was much more than an eclectic
throwing together of unlike elements. The *Liber maiolichus,*

written in 1135 to celebrate the expedition against the Saracens in the Balearic Islands, referred to Pisa as the 'second Rome' and drew attention to the major policy role assumed by the city on that occasion. Analogously, the stylistic wealth resulting from voyages and commercial and diplomatic ties with areas from the Orient to the Rhine valley was managed with a sense of responsibility previously unknown in the West. It was a study that by-passed Graeco-Roman intellectual norms – incomprehensible until the Renaissance – and settled instead on the repertory of distributive and constructive models codified in antiquity: composition as a sum of equal elements whose Pythagorean references were in fact given theoretical expression by the Pisan mathematician Leonardo Fibonacci (1202). The centrality of this experience is demonstrated by the prestige of Pisan models and their spread over a vast area: Sicily, Sardinia, Apulia, and Tuscany, where it became one of the bases for the subsequent Florentine Renaissance.

As the city took shape, so did the remarkable group of religious buildings in its north-west corner. The cathedral was begun in 1063 by Buschetto, while the Sicilian expedition in support of the Normans was under way (a fact recorded in an inscription on the façade), and consecrated in 1118, twenty years after the First Crusade. Immediately afterwards it was extended by Rainaldo, and the new façade was completed with the bronze doors of Bonanno in 1180. The structure carries obvious signs of this alteration: the joints of the supporting frame are grafted one above the other in a way puzzling at least to those who seek to justify this situation on the basis of knowledge not equal to the scale of the problem.

Construction of the baptistery (1152) and the tower (1173) began in the period of Pisa's greatest political success, when the entire Tyrrhenian coast from Portovenere to Civitavecchia (1162) and Sardinia (1165) were received in fee from Frederick I. These structures created around the cathedral a collection of separate monuments placed in an open space, an exceptional arrangement in medieval Italy which owed its logic to the same repetitive scheme found in the buildings themselves. It was a scheme that allowed the addition of other isolated elements, like the Campo Santo (cemetery) begun in 1278. In 1286 a law made the surrounding space for ever free of other buildings.

It may be that this complex, located on the edge of the existing city, was in fact an uncompleted project intended to be the centre

15 *Pisa Cathedral, Baptistery and Leaning Tower in 1931 (photo: Alinari, no. 8571).*

of a new city of unimaginably grand scale and dignity. The existing situation of four monuments placed together in an open and grassy area dizzily amplifies the effects of the repetition of similar elements on different volumes, prismatic and curved, which are superimposed in an infinite number of ways ('unité dans le détail, tumulte dans l'ensemble' as Corbusier wrote in 1934).[4] The leaning of the tower – perhaps intended from the outset as De Angelis d'Ossat supposes[5] – lets us glimpse even a degree of freedom from the universal obligation of verticality, a concept which we have in fact lost.

Leaving the ecclesiastical buildings isolated at its north-western corner, the city follows the course of the Arno, with its double line of palazzi of equal height on either side, its embankments and stairways to the river, and the outer fortifications of the citadel and arsenal forming a continuous space curved like a bow, all visible in a single glance. In the Renaissance no other river city in Europe could equal it; today the view is spoiled by the great walls built in 1870.

On the eve of the crisis caused by the defeat of Meloria (1284), the enigmatic personality of Nicola Pisano, perhaps *'de Apulia'*, appeared on the scene. His conscious revival of the ancient sculptural tradition can be viewed as either an original development of classicism in the age of Frederick or else a consequence of the responsiveness developed in Pisa regarding the Classical legacy (consider the true archaeological collection put together in the galleries of the Campo Santo in those years). In any case, his contribution was decisive for the artistic culture of Italy, and the work of his followers – who included Arnolfo da Cambio and Giovanni Pisano, leaders in Florentine and Sienese sculpture – is to be found in all parts of the peninsula.

Pisa was, however, cut off from the great events that followed. In the first years of the fourteenth century, the Kinsica quarter south of the Arno was enclosed within the city walls, bringing the total size to 185 hectares, but after the plague of mid-century, the population of the city declined as malaria spread in the countryside and the port silted up. In 1406 Pisa fell to the Florentines, who dedicated their efforts to the new port of Livorno to the south, and in the sixteenth century its population was reduced to 8,600 inhabitants.

The wonderful medieval city, for a time the virtual capital of the Mediterranean, a synthesis of east and west, became afterwards a quiet provincial centre, as had previously happened to Ravenna. The prestigious and enigmatic monuments, spread throughout the city and surrounding countryside and made ever more a part of the latter by events, remain as testimony of a highly developed figurative culture, superseded by and made obsolete by 'modern' classicism.

Genoa, rival and later conqueror of Pisa, established its port and urban framework on a narrow strip of coast virtually cut off from inland areas. Traces of the Roman city are hard to find, and a definitive urban plan first took shape in the ninth century as Genoa adopted an important role in the Carolingian state. The walls of 864 enclosed 22 hectares, including the Castello hill, and part of the small plain to the north, where the bishop's see and cathedral moved in the tenth century. Only three gates opened to the surrounding hills – San Pietro to the north, Castello to the south,

16   Genoa in the late sixteenth century (from a painting in the Vatican Map Gallery (photo: Anderson, no. 41559).

and Soprana to the east, where after the battle of Meloria the chain taken from the port of Pisa was hung – while the western side facing the sea was equipped for the business of the port. The orthogonal design of the flat areas, although reminiscent of a Roman plan, should be considered a new organism deriving from the same logic as in Pisa.

The walls of 1155–61, which defined the city throughout the medieval period, expanded the city to 65 hectares, encompassing all of the plain including the *borgo* of San Siro up to the slopes of the surrounding hills. The most important functions were all performed in an arc of structures, carefully organized by the municipal authorities, which faced on to the port and include the city hall of 1260. It was 'an international infrastructure which served as a hinge between two differently scaled systems: that of local trade and the territorial system of trade throughout the entire Tyrrhenian and Mediterranean areas'.[6] In 1139 the coastal strip was made state property. The city's extraordinary waterfront was completed by the breakwater and two lighthouses of the twelfth century, the Ripa porticoes and warehouses, the city hall of 1260 projecting from the arc of buildings and the late thirteenth-century arsenal outside the walls. Together these structures established the man-made setting for Genoa's gigantic commercial and military expansion and successful competition with Venice until 1380.

In this tightly packed city open spaces are rare: the small cathedral churchyard and the *curiae* where the houses of the principal aristocratic families were found, like that of the Doria family next to the Church of San Matteo (rebuilt in 1278). The city was divided into eight converging segments or *comapagnie* which form a fan along the line of the coast. The anchorage, poorly protected by the *molo vecchio* (breakwater), stretched out to the west toward Monte San Benigno. This hill would be crowned, in 1543, with the tall Lanterna Tower and its slopes terraced with Renaissance and Baroque villas and modern fortifications right up to the ridge.

This splendid work of practical architecture, planned by the community, acquired its character from the material and mental economy employed in its construction, from the rejection of superfluity, and from the rigorous selection of artistic styles; it guaranteed the good fortune of Genoa for many years. The city lost political independence in the sixteenth century, but remained

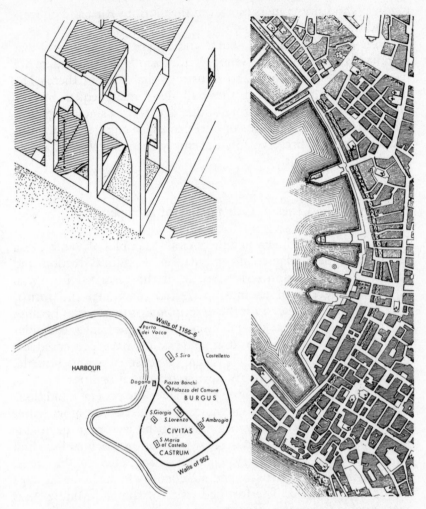

17   *The Ripa Maris, Genoa: reconstruction of the twelfth-century con-struction work (from L. Grossi-Bianchi and E. Poleggi,* Una città portuale del Medievo, *Genoa: SAGEP, 1980); the waterfront in an 1883 map.*

wealthy and securely integrated with the inland areas. This new economic role, severely at odds with the history of the city, assaulted the old setting and today has rendered it unrecognizable. The modern port is a workshop bristling with gigantic machines, closed by a wall which cuts off the front of the city; elevated roadways and skyscrapers block out the glorious Ripa and oppress its traditional dimensions.

While Pisa – like Athens, Rome and Bruges – is a large city that commands a nearby port, Genoa, Venice and later Amsterdam are blended with their ports and indistinguishable from them. The maritime installations and the buildings, made equal by the empirical and inventive culture of that age, form a single organism which defies the distinctions of our specialized culture. In fact, our age seems able to preserve only the empty corpse of Venice, and of Genoa not even that.

Cities in Other Parts of Europe

In the three extraordinary and precocious examples of Venice, Pisa and Genoa, the fundamental combination of political freedom and spatial experimentation characteristic of the medieval European city found several of its most perfected functional and formal expressions. We began with the description of these cities because the transition from a general discussion to particular examples would have been less evocative and would have prevented us, distant descendants, from expressing a sense of wonder at the appearance of these singularly new architectural realities.

At this point we should stop to consider the general conditions that made similar results possible in hundreds of other cities throughout Europe. At the beginning of the European demographic expansion, a portion of the new population was unable to find employment in the countryside and so migrated to the cities, swelling the ranks of artisans and merchants who lived on the edge of the feudal world. The fortified cities of the late Middle Ages were unable to contain all of this population, and new settlements formed outside the gates, quickly gaining equal footing with the original centres and so requiring the building of ever-expanded city walls. The artisan and merchant population of these expanded cities formed a majority from the start and sought to move away from the feudal political system in order to ensure favourable conditions for their economic activities. These conditions included an autonomous administration and judiciary, and a system of taxes proportional to income to be used for works of general public utility, especially fortifications and armaments.

Out of the clash with bishops and princes, these new organizations were transformed from private associations to communes in which power was public and the prerogatives of the particular individual or group were subjugated to those of the community, while still maintaining respect for economic privilege. The organs of city government, which foreshadowed those of the modern state, almost always consisted of a high council which represented the most important private interests, a subordinate council which functioned as an executive committee, and a number of elected or randomly selected magistrates (the *consoli* in Italy, the *jurés* in France, the *échevins* in Flanders). Balancing these were the associations which represented portions of the citizenry, the corporations (*arti* in Italy, *Zünfte* in Germany, guilds in England), and the companies under arms, which chose their own magistrate, the *capitano del popolo*. Parallel to the civil authorities were the religious: the priests and, after the thirteenth century, the monastic orders based in the city. In Italy a visiting magistrate, the *podestà*, was occasionally called in to arbitrate conflicts between political bodies and social classes.

This autonomous arrangement extended only to the edge of the city and not to the countryside beyond. The city depended on the countryside for a supply of necessary goods, and in fact controlled an area of varying size, but, as opposed to the Greek *polis*, it was a 'closed' city and did not concede equal rights to the inhabitants of the countryside. Economic and political relationships might exist on a global scale, but they were managed according to the interests of a restricted urban population. As with the assemblies of the Greek cities, even this limited body did not always express itself with one voice. The dominant classes, represented in the councils, became progressively larger, but never so large as to include salaried workers. When the latter engaged in the battle for power – during the economic crisis of the second half of the fourteenth century – they always lost, with the result that power was concentrated in the hands of a few families or even a single dominant family. The visible manifestation of these conflicts was the competition for advantageous or even speculative occupation of urban space, competition only partially regulated by institutional rules.

The above description applies to a variety of concrete experiences which are not otherwise reducible to general models nor supported by general theoretical considerations. European medieval cities did not enjoy 'freedom', but 'freedoms'; they were not characterized by abstract institutional categories, but institutions devised to suit each particular concrete situation. The physical form of the city depended upon the political organization, which was in turn made possible by this setting. It was a setting which served as a stage for the meetings and conflicts of many players, an image holding interest for all and one in which to recognize and be recognized. Out of the multiplicity of its structures we can identify four constituent innovations:

1 The unrestricted concentration of public and private buildings made up an integrated and highly personalized organism which presented a summary and easily read external façade. The medieval city may seem 'irregular' to us because it is not based on a large-scale geometric plan like those used in both ancient and Renaissance cities. It relies instead on the perfect adaptation of its various elements, added one after another at different points in time. Streets and squares create a unique and well-constructed environment in which every player has his part and the community finds its identity. The streets come in different shapes and serve a series of collective and non-specialized functions: for the movement of pedestrians and carts; as places of rest; and for markets, meetings and celebrations. The squares provide spaces which, though larger, respond to the same conceptual needs as the streets. The buildings, almost always several stories tall, face out on to this complex system as a compact mass, their façades forming the walls of the public space (in Venice it is instead the canals which make up the polyvalent public space, while the passageways on the islands serve only for foot traffic and were not combined into a continuous network until the nineteenth century). A mechanism of this sort forced private interests to co-operate on the fitting out of public spaces: a façade, the means by which a building presents itself, becomes also 'a gift to the street',[7] a contribution to the functioning and splendour of the urban environment. Medieval statutes did, in fact, carefully regulate this interface between the public and private worlds, dictating the smallest details of the compromise between competing interests. This was especially true for those areas where the two overlapped: outcroppings which covered a part of the street, porticoes, external staircases.

2   Complexity was another characteristic common to both the social body and the physical setting. The structure of urban public space was the result of a balance between different centres of power: the bishopric, the civil government, religious orders, guilds, and social classes. Larger cities were never characterized by a single centre; instead they included a religious centre, a political centre and one or more commercial centres, often bordering one on the other but none the less in opposition to some degree. Every city was divided into *quartiers*, *sestieri*, *rioni*, boroughs or wards possessing their own organization and symbols, and often a degree of political autonomy. In the expansions of the thirteenth century the monasteries of mendicant orders – Franciscans, Dominicans, Augustinians, Servites – served as secondary centres to the cities where they carried out their mission.

3   A consequence of the closed and privileged character of the medieval city was density: the city occupied as restricted an area as possible within which the most sought-after locations were in the centre; buildings grew taller and the city's general profile came to be dominated by public structures – churches, city halls – and their generally vertical development. The most expensive public project was the building of city walls, indispensable for defence (except in Venice), which followed the shortest possible outline to enclose a given surface area. The building of new walls was put off as long as possible, until the old circle was jammed completely full. Only the later expansions undertaken shortly before the crises of the fourteenth century (in Florence, Siena, Bologna, Verona, Padua, Ghent, Louvain and Cologne) were not filled, and included open cultivated spaces for many centuries afterward. This new relationship between horizontal extension and height contributed to the perception of the city as a physical entity extending in all three dimensions; it provided a precise and concrete image in support of the collective identity of the citizens, finding its place in nature but easily distinguished from it. The painters of the thirteenth and fourteenth centuries were both active participants in this setting and the agents of its representation.

4   The dynamic character of medieval urban development made for a continual state of non-completion which we conjure up with difficulty because we are accustomed to the later definitive size of the cities, established between the fifteenth and eighteenth centuries. In the Middle Ages, churches and public buildings were often

construction sites, covered with scaffolding, and completed houses alternated with those being built; each project represented a new and surprising addition. Coherent rules of style, a guide for the future rather than a memory of the past, guaranteed unity of composition. The search for a set of rules that would be rational, fixed and flexible all at the same time made headway in the second half of the twelfth century when the work of a group of patrons and builders in the Ile-de-France created an international decorative and constructive style that would later be called Gothic.

Analysis of the vaulted stone structures was carried out so far as to establish a rigorous distinction between the three-dimensional supporting framework and the supported elements, upsetting the continuity of the surrounding walls; continuity between the various constructive elements was established within this framework which made constant reference to the project as a whole. Each element carried the imprint of its placement within the overall system to which it remained subordinate. Use of the pointed arch was essential for this purpose as it freed the top of the arch from its span and permitted the fixing of its height independently of the distance between its abutments. The series of church bays were in this way combined into a continuous space, and the ceiling rose in order to balance the dimensions not of the bays but of the entire church. The form and decoration of each element could be reinvented anew, and this situation inspired a drawn-out search for perfection that would be resolved only by means of Renaissance normalization and reference back to Classical models.

The spread of the Gothic repertory from the first half of the thirteenth century provided a method for bringing the ever more rapid and extensive urban changes under control, establishing for the first time a unified European architectural language, parallel to the role played by Latin in theological scholasticism today. While still maintaining a high degree of diversity, the cities of Europe became identifiable as the products of a single and self-conscious civilization.

The survey necessary to illustrate this discussion properly would be considerably longer than this entire book; it can be summarized by identifying the following regions:

I That area of the Mediterranean urbanized in the Classical age – northern and central Italy and southern France – where almost all cities developed according to a pre-existing Roman plan (though, in addition to Venice, other important new cities were founded, like the diked city of Ferrara).

II Southern Italy and Spain, where the reconquest of previously Arab and Byzantine territories required a closer confrontation with earlier urban models.

III The area between the Loire and the Rhine, Germany, England, and the Scandinavian and Slavic countries, where the traces of Roman settlements were rarer or non-existent so that few cities conformed to the classical pattern, most being founded in this period according to an original design.

I

The initial design of the previously Roman cities – already substantially altered both in terms of construction and overall balance – generally supplied a neutral geometric base, the grid, for the new urban functions. The commercial zone was usually unchanged and coincided with the forum (Lucca, Florence, Bologna, Padua, Lyon). In the peripheral areas, the new political and religious centres were often established astride the ancient walls, where it was easier to find the space necessary for their activities. The design of roads converging on the gates was repeated in the settlements that grew up around the walls, and then again as the cities expanded. The resulting organisms, in which rotations and angled connections complicated the transit structures, were of singular complexity.

These processes emerge with diagrammatic clarity in Bologna, which lies on a plain and whose shape is not determined by an important river. Inhabited since the remote past, the ancient city was the site of one of the largest colonial cities of northern Italy, comprising 70 hectares and a population of several tens of thousands. In the late Middle Ages, the city occupied only the southwest corner of the Roman quadrilateral, enclosed by a wall in the sixth century; it was expanded by the Lombards outside the Ravegnana gate and equipped with a semicircular wall which

18   *Bologna (engraving by C. Duchet, 1592).*

protected the ray of streets from the plain to the east. In 1019 the *extra moenia* cathedral was transferred to the southern edge of the city, where it still stands today. The famous university, the oldest in Europe, was founded in 1088 and received in trust the Justinian Pandects from Ravenna. The Commune, in which the Latin and Lombard cities were combined, was created after the death of Countess Matilda in 1115. By the end of the twelfth century the city had tripled in size to 120 hectares and boasted a new circle of walls (1055–70) which included all of the Roman quadrilateral and a semicircular appendage to the east. In 1201 the Commune definitively established its seat in the centre of the ancient nucleus, and in the second half of that century began the construction of an immense third circle of walls, completed in 1380, which expanded the urban area in all directions and included a second ray of roads to the west converging on the San Felice gate (about 450 hectares). The walled perimeter intercepted the roads of the two rays at a greater or lesser distance from their starting-point according to scale of construction along them, and serves as a diagram of their varying importance, that is of the relationship between the city and

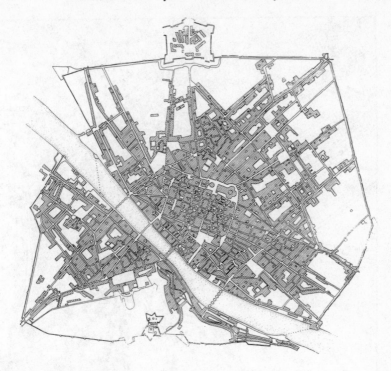

19   *Map of Florence as it was in 1783.*

the surrounding territory. Beginning in 1211, a series of laws governed construction of the porticoes that flank the city streets and stretch for a total of 38 kilometres.

The development of Florence is yet another example of the utilization of a pre-existing design. Florentia was a Roman city of secondary importance, oriented according to the points of the compass but aligned with neither the property divisions of the surrounding countryside nor with the River Arno; this placement would be a determining factor in its subsequent development. The Carolingian city included the southern part of the Roman rectangle as well as a triangle that abutted the river. In the eleventh century, urban growth reoccupied the northern part beyond the old forum, which had always been located at the intersection of the principal axes, and began to extend beyond the four gates. Between 1173 and 1175 the Commune, established here also in 1115, built the 'ancient

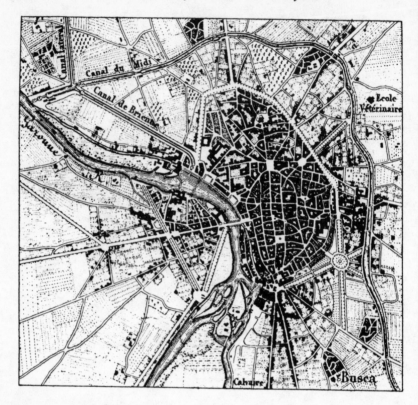

20   *Map of Toulouse in 1841 (Duclos).*

circle' of walls described by Dante which enclosed this organism and was rotated relative to the earlier walls in order to include the settlements which had since grown up around it on either side of the river. In the following century, the city – by now one of the most important manufacturing and financial centres of Europe with about 100,000 inhabitants – grew beyond this perimeter as well and required a true regulatory plan, supervised by Arnolfo da Cambio. The centre and the periphery were redesigned in tandem. Behind the original nucleus, both a religious centre – the new cathedral of Santa Maria del Fiore – and a political centre – the Palazzo and Piazza della Signoria – were established. In anticipation of further growth a great new circle of walls encompassing 480 hectares was planned, again rotated relative to the previous one, and for the same reason. It was on this splendid canvas that the artists of the Renaissance would work to perfect the urban form of the fifteenth and sixteenth centuries.

In many other cases the existence of a river influenced the development of a Roman grid city, rendering the initial design secondary. On the banks of the Garonne, Toulouse, already made capital of the Visigoths in 419, became the most important metropolis of southern France and was about to become its own city-state on a level with the great communes of Italy when the Albigensian Crusade (1226–8) ended its autonomy. The Roman nucleus and its appendages – the Bourg on the western side, with the famous statue of Saint-Sernin, and the Saint-Cyprien quarter across the river – were enclosed by a stone wall in about the year 1140, and four bridges spanning the Garonne were built between 1152 and 1284. The wall of brick finished in stone united the vast setting on either side of the river and tied together its important monuments: the Churches of Saint-Étienne and Saint-Sernin and the Jacobin convent.

In many river cities – Bordeaux, Tours, Cologne – the organism evolved analogously from a quadrilateral form to a semicircular one abutting on the river. In others, founded at the confluence of two rivers – Koblenz, Lyon – or else in a river's sharp bend – Verona – the framework established on the peninsula in Roman times was preserved with particular precision and the enlargements made either at the base of the peninsula or across the river were clearly distinct from the original nucleus.

In hilly areas, obedience to the terrain overthrew the regularity of any pre-existing design and placed a natural limit on the size of the urban organism. In the Apennines, in the Alps and in the French Massif Central many medium-size cities were founded on defensible elevations. In at least one case, this situation did not impede the development of a great city, comparable in size and importance to those described above: Siena.

The original Etruscan and Roman city occupied a site not particularly favourable from a geographical or topographical point of view. None the less, it became important in the late Middle Ages when the Via Flaminia was blocked by the Lombard occupation, and both the Roman coastal roads and the stretch of the Via Cassia in the Val di Chiana turned to swamp. The first medieval city, established by Rotaris in the seventh century, occupied the two hills of Castelvecchio and Santa Maria, where the cathedral was

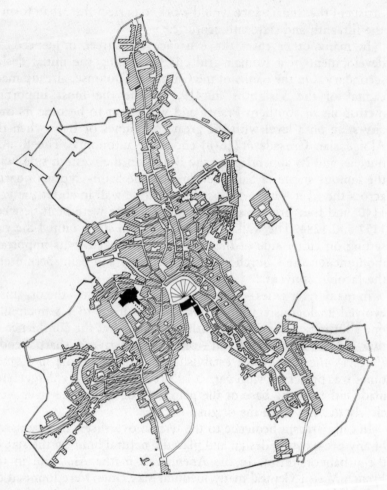

21 Map of Siena in 1848.

placed. To the east of this nucleus ran the Via Roma along a ridge line which witnessed a multiplication of settlements in both directions. The great communal city grew out of this constellation at the end of the eleventh century. It preserved the original outline in the division into *terzi* (thirds) – that of the Città, which included the ancient nucleus, of Camollia around the northern ridge, and of San Martino around the southern ridge – subdivided then into the seventeen *contrade*.

22 Siena: *aerial view showing the cathedral and Piazza del Campo (photo: Fotocielo, no. 15/197).*

The top of the Santa Maria hill was enlarged to support the cathedral, whose spires crown the profile of the city. Its black and white striped exterior gives this great building exceptional prominence and visual primacy over all the surrounding countryside. The indentation south of the intersection of the roads running along the ridges was transformed by the construction of the city hall (Palazzo Pubblico) facing up the incline and the demarcation of the vast upward-sloping concavity before it: the Campo, where the open space of the community faces the constructed seat of the public magistrates in unsurpassed architectural rapport.

The conscious modelling of the Campo terrain engenders a superb transfiguration: the curving bell-shaped profile of the uphill semicircle of buildings and the sharp straight-line course, slightly broken, of the downhill Palazzo embrace the scallop shell pavement divided into nine unequal sectors converging on a great drain in front of the Palazzo. The towering campanile, planned in 1325, placed at the eastern corner of the Palazzo and supported by a chapel facing the piazza, serves a complex function: it corrects the off-centre placement (to the west) of the Palazzo; it stands out from the openness of the piazza; and it competes with the mass of the cathedral in the view of Siena from afar, like a gigantic pivot between the interior and exterior of the city. Its jagged peak of grey stone balanced on top of the smooth trunk of brick draws the threads of the great community environment together and aloft, a signal to the surrounding landscape in all directions.

A qualitative accomplishment of this sort, which has few peers, must of course incorporate a series of important individual contributions. It is supposed that Giovanni Pisano, master builder of the cathedral works from 1284 to 1295, had a hand, and Duccio, the great leader of Sienese painting (active until 1319), was consulted on a number of points. Statutes of 1262 and 1297, revealing an acute sense of the delicate rapport between public and private needs in this crucial location, prescribed in detail the necessary characteristics of the buildings facing the Campo and its allowable (and prohibited) uses.

The circle of walls enclosing the Y formed by the ridges on which the city was built was erected around 1150; it was subsequently expanded in 1220, 1260 and 1326, including sections of the surrounding slopes and contours for a total area of 180 hectares, not much less than the great plain cities. Siena was later sorely tested by the plague of the fourteenth century and fell in battle to the Florentines who were ousted only in 1555. Its subsequent history up to the present day has been conditioned by the inconsistency of this grandiose construction, which corresponds neither to the size nor the resources of the city and stands as testimony to one human group's paradoxical challenge to an environment which was as a result reinvented.

II

In those territories which remained for a long period under Byzantine rule – the coastal regions of southern Italy and the Balkan peninsula – urban growth was checked and the defensive contraction of the early centuries remained a permanent characteristic. Byzantine administrations gradually dismantled several of the major Graeco-Roman cities – Brindisi, Taranto, Syracuse, Agrigento, Athens, Corinth – concentrating the population in a small, easily defensible area – the areas around Ortygia in Syracuse, the acropolis structures of Agrigento and Athens – while several inland cities located in particularly rugged areas gained prominence – Matera, Enna, Mistra. The Arabs conquered Syracuse in 848. A letter written by the monk Theodosius describes with great emotion this great event which deleted one of the great capitals of the ancient world from the geography of Europe.

The Arabs occupied Sicily for a century and a half, long threatening the coastal cities of southern Italy: Siponto was occupied in 927, Taranto in 976 and Rome itself was sacked in 846. The Byzantines none the less held Calabria and Apulia until the end of the eleventh century; Bari was occupied by the Normans in 1071. The long domination of the Greeks left an indelible mark on the centres lining the Apulian coast and outweighed that of later transformations under Norman and Swabian rule. The Hautevilles and the Hohenstaufens continuously shifted their residences, creating individual civil and religious monuments in many cities while not significantly modifying any of them in the long run.

The reconquest, while it left many Byzantine cities in their marginal position awarded new political and economic importance to a number of ports in Campania – Salerno, Naples – and so appropriate physical development as well. Naples emerged as the permanent capital of the southern kingdom, inheriting an urban plan already important in ancient times in the centre of an area which had always been densely populated.

In the late Middle Ages, Naples remained a city of landowners and occupied only a part of the Graeco-Roman site enclosed by a circle of walls in the tenth and eleventh centuries. Afterwards, it gradually expanded to include the area between these walls and the sea, so that next to the regular Hippodamian pattern another irregular and fragmented pattern emerged, resembling the Arab prototype. Charles of Anjou, who made Naples his capital in 1266, added a series of important structures – the castle at the western edge of the anchorage, the market, the southern walls, a breakwater for the port and the church of San Lorenzo (with an ambulatory apse in the French style) – and also an autonomous administration based on the system of *sedili* (districts), a decidedly northern touch. In this way, 'One of the oldest western cities . . . became one of the primary capitals of that monarchical Europe coming into existence at the end of the thirteenth century; it was modelled on Paris . . . but owed much to the heritage of Frederick II.'[8] The grid formed by the three major level streets (*decumani*) and by the many upward-sloping cross streets hosted the accumulation of a multitude of heterogeneous structures, a process which would continue for centuries without sacrificing the city's eloquent readability.

Those Italian and Spanish cities reconquered from the Arabs, though often of Graeco-Roman origin, were of an entirely diffe-rent measure and had undergone profound modification during the Islamic occupation, the period of their greatest development and prosperity. Their structure – one of contiguous enclosures in which the buildings faced central courtyards while the residual space served as a communication network – was well adapted to the inclusion of inhabited and cultivated spaces so as to form an agglomeration of great extent: covering vast areas, Palermo reached a population of several hundred thousand and Cordoba perhaps half a million.

The Christian crusaders inherited these organisms from a weal-thier and more evolved society and, reusing them according to their own requirements and with more limited resources, in some sense went through that same separation from the Classical tradition described above. The contrasting needs of continuity, concentration and detachment from the countryside emerged as a result. This undertaking challenged for the first time the originality of Western culture and produced several of its most intriguing urban settings, in which the contributions of two heterogeneous cultures are combined in surprising ways. From another point of view, it was the first large-scale squandering of the heritage of a foreign culture which, in the process of its assimilation, was drastically impoverished. The crusaders themselves recognized this loss to some degree and attempted to compensate for it through the preservation of several monumental structures: the Arab structures in the park of William II in Palermo and the great Mosque of Cordoba, which was partially altered only in the sixteenth century.

Palermo, conquered by the Normans in 1072, is a great metro-polis set into the Conca d'Oro semicircle of hills. The slightly raised ancient city and its port were surrounded by settlements spread over a large area and fed by both natural and artificial streams coming from the hinterland. The new ruling class was small and occupied a few strategic points of the city. Near the hills and connected to the cathedral by the *via coperta* (covered way) was the citadel; the kings took up residence in this splendid and exotic organism, basis of the state's wealth. Over the following centuries, adaptation to European rules was gradually achieved; these included more compact construction – the elimination of internal enclosures and the building of an external surrounding wall, consolidated in several phases – and the substitution of a new multi-level outward-facing building style for the previous low inward-facing blocks. The green spaces that formed part of the city were progressively filled, though several of unaccustomed size – the open space in front of the Palazzo, Piazza Marina, the top of the Papireto – remained to give Palermo that regal character which it maintains even in its current state of ruin.

This sort of hybridization, which gives Palermo special prestige among Italian cities, is instead a standard characteristic of the majority of Spanish cities. Barcelona, occupied by the Arabs in 713 but early reconquered by the Franks in 801, became – after the last Arab invasion of 985 – an important centre of trade in the western Mediterranean and enjoyed development analogous to that of the Italian maritime cities and Marseille. The urban enclosure encompassed approximately the 100 hectares of the Roman model, partially altered in the Arab period. The Aragon kings made an addition in 1350, but this only gradually filled with houses. As in many other European cities the expanded city was characterized by an irregular transportation system that followed the extra-urban roads.

More radical transformations, before and after reconquest, occurred in those cities where Islamic rule held for a longer period of time. Toledo had been the Visigoth capital until occupied by the Arabs in 712; it was retaken by the Christians in 1085 and became the capital of the kingdoms of Castille and León. Its mountainous setting impeded the straightening and enlarging of streets usual in other cities – Valencia, Almeria – and the building of houses several stories high facing on to the streets led to an alarming congestion of public space. Ordinances required that projections should not extend over more than one-third of the street's width on either side, which left the central one-third for the passage of air, light and rain. The most important public buildings – the

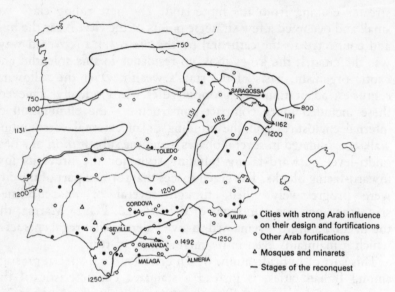

23   Phases in the reconquest of Spain, showing Arab cities (from C. T. Smith, An Historical Geography of Western Europe before 1800, 1967).

Alcazar built immediately after the reconquest, and the Gothic cathedral begun in 1227 – extend upward and can be seen in their entirety only from a distance because of the narrowness of the surrounding spaces. The distinct character of the city, summed up in its unique external appearance, derives from these factors.

The cities of Andalusia were reconquered later – Cordoba in 1236, Seville in 1248 and Granada only in 1492 – and preserve still more strongly their Arab character. In these, entire quarters of low short houses survive (well adapted to the region's climate): 'All the architecture is within the body of the houses; little care is devoted to the exterior.'[9] The Christians respected and preserved the principal monuments left by the Muslims – the Mosque of Cordoba, the Giralda of Seville, the Royal Palace of Granada – and the coexistence of contrasting cultural influences would remain a lasting characteristic of these urban settings. When Spain conquered an overseas colonial empire, using Seville as its logistic centre, these composite environments were reproduced with surprising results, even in the remote territories of Mexico and Peru.

24a   Toledo: painting by El Greco (El Greco Museum, Toledo; photo: Anderson, no. 16995).

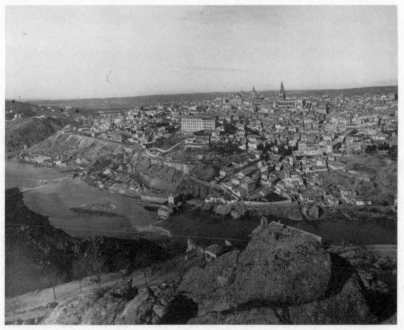

24b   Toledo today (photo: Ministerio de Informacion y Turismo, Archivio Fotografico, ref. 46, no. 279).

25   *Granada: part of the Albaicín, from the Alhambra (photo: Bene-volo).*

III

In northern Europe, the distinction between cities based on previously existing ancient organisms – Trier, Cologne, Mainz, Augsburg, London – and those born of an original design loses importance. Environmental conditions and new techniques of construction, in particular the use of wood, affected the varieties of planimetric outline.

The Roman city situated on the raised left bank of the Seine was only one of several elements that would constitute Paris. In the first half of the twelfth century this capital expanded as the two settlements of Grève and Saint-Germain-l'Auxerrois, together with the Champeau market, appeared on the right bank. The island Cité, the right-bank commercial centre and the left-bank university formed a coherent organism which Philippe Auguste completed by adding Les Halles (1186), a circle of walls (1180–1210) and the Louvre fortress on the river. Around 1370, Charles X expanded the semicircle of walls on the right bank, occupying the greater

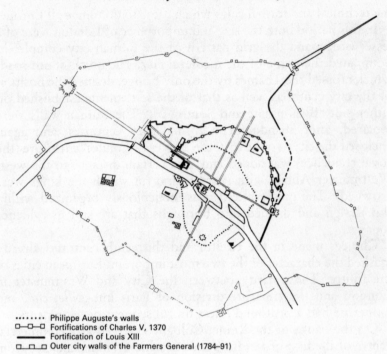

········ Philippe Auguste's walls
□—□—□ Fortifications of Charles V, 1370
———— Fortification of Louis XIII
□ □ □ Outer city walls of the Farmers General (1784–91)

26   *Paris, showing the successive city perimeters (from L. Bergeron, ed., Paris, Genèse d'un paysage, Paris: Picard, 1989).*

part of that half-moon between the Seine and the surrounding arc of swamps which had already been frequented in pre-Roman times. The fortified walls of the sixteenth century and the *grands boulevards* of the seventeenth would follow this fundamental pattern, still perfectly discernible in the city today.

The total area of the city, based on a new political and cultural role, came to 440 hectares. The lovely white stone taken from the left-bank quarries or the Val d'Oise and cut into uniform blocks added an element of unity to the great civil and religious structures, the most significant of which was the new cathedral of Notre-Dame rebuilt between 1163 and 1250. The intellectual leadership of Paris found its centre in the university, where Abélard and Bernard discussed the great problems of the day, but also in many sectors of religious and civil life: for our purposes the structural inventions of Suger and the Ile-de-France masters was decisive and established the technical and formal rules which came to dominate all Europe.

In this period both the size and importance of London were of a lesser order, and the grid pattern of the Roman city completely dominated the shape of the medieval city. The north–south road, which crossed the Thames by the only bridge, defined the position of the city centre as well as that of the settlements established on either side, Bishopsgate and Southwark. The Roman walls were repaired, after abandonment in the early centuries, and again enclosed the city. To the east, the Tower of London enclosure (the royal residence) was added and, at a certain distance to the west, Westminster Abbey with its cathedral (in which the kings were crowned). The medieval city was meticulously organized within this design and divided into boroughs that are still in evidence today.

Choices made in the twelfth and thirteenth centuries already marked the character of the two most important European cities of the future. The polarity between the City and Westminster in London and the tripartite division of Paris into *ville*, *cité*, and *université* had a profound effect on subsequent developments.

On the banks of the Rhine, Cologne emerged as a commercial centre of the first order; for a time it achieved independence from the rule of the bishops, establishing an autonomous organization. Cologne had been an important Roman city of about 100 hectares; it was reduced to an agricultural settlement by the Franks and destroyed by the Normans in 881. The commercial centre subsequently developed by extending the Roman walls to the river and then absorbing the surrounding settlements in two successive enclosures, in 1106 and 1180, which expanded the city to 200 and then 450 hectares. The Romanesque and Ottonian churches – St Pantaleon, St Maria im Kapitol, St Gereon, the Church of the Holy Apostles, and St Martin – are characterized by complex planimetry, and their varied profiles stand out from the urban setting. The Gothic cathedral, begun in 1248 to house the relics of the Magi taken from Milan by Frederick Barbarossa, dominates from a small elevation the long stretch of the city facing the river (too wide to be spanned by a bridge).

The cities in Flanders and along the northern coast of Germany, where textile industries and the northern commercial ports operated free from the direct influence of the courts, achieved in time political autonomy and an international economic role similar to

27   Cologne (engraving by Braun and Hogenberg, 1582).

that of the cities of northern and central Italy. These were the trading centres and castles mentioned in the previous chapter which developed gradually, eventually becoming great cities. Their names are indicative of their origin in open territory – 'Bruges' means bridge, 'Leuven' (Louvain) a hill rising out of the heath, 'Brussels' a village in the swamp – and their curvilinear plans, guided by the waterways, are entirely independent of ancient orthogonal geometry.

Bruges, the largest mercantile city north of the Alps, developed around a fortified castle on the River Reye built by the Flemish counts at the end of the ninth century. The river flowed into an arm of the sea which extended far inland; on its banks the first commercial settlement, the *portus*, was established and the first fair took place in 957. Other small settlements formed around the churches on the higher points of the swampy plain. In the eleventh century Bruges acquired the right of self-government from its feudal lord and established its own magistrates. The city grew, and a first circle of walls encompassed an area of 86 hectares and a population of about 10,000.

In 1134 a storm changed the shape of the coast and created a deep gulf, the Zwyn, at the end of the inlet mentioned above. The

28   *Bruges (engraving by L. Guicciardini, in* Descrizione di tutti i Paesi Bassi, *1567).*

merchants of Bruges moved quickly to exploit this natural port, barely a mile outside the city. They built a new harbour, Damme, on the Zwyn and a canal connecting it to the Reye and to the city. In the following century Bruges became the primary continental landing on the North Sea. Commercial relations with the Hanseatic League were negotiated in 1252 and with England – which supplied wool to Flemish industry – by the 1274 Treaty of Montreuil, in accordance with which Edward I established that wool exported to the Continent had to pass through Bruges. In 1277 the first Genoese galleys arrived in the Zwyn, followed shortly afterward by the Venetians. In the fourteenth century Bruges was connected to Venice by a daily overland postal service.

A new circle of walls encompassing 430 hectares was begun in 1297 and completed in the middle of the fourteenth century. The municipal administration was housed inside the Castle in the old Halle, though the city's activities focused on the large square located at the *portus*, site of the new city hall with its tall belfry built between 1377 and 1420. The Waterhalle was built over the

29   Bruges: part of the medieval quarter, from the belfry of the town hall (photo: Benevolo).

30   Bruges: the canal between the city and outer harbour (photo: Benevolo).

river at the end of the thirteenth century (and destroyed at the end of the eighteenth); there ships could enter and be loaded or unloaded under cover. A huge open space for the fairs was maintained at the city's western edge. In the first half of the thirteenth century the population may have reached 80,000.

The stylistic coherence of the urban organism depends again on a repeated scheme of building, different from that of Venice but equally well adapted to the curving canals and roads: a succession of gable-topped load-bearing walls parallel to the streets with perpendicular steeply sloping roof pitches which allowed for the illumination of the façade insets from above and gave the urban outline its characteristic toothed appearance. In the last decades of the thirteenth century the government dedicated a third of its resources to public works – city walls, paving, water supply – and carefully regulated private building: roofs were to be tiled (to avoid fires) and the city paid one-third of the expenses; the owners of buildings to be demolished for the widening of streets were compensated, but demolition on one's own initiative was not permitted unless rebuilding took place within four months.

Economic crisis and civil war weakened Bruges in the late fourteenth century. The Zwyn was silting up and the harbour had to be moved from Damme to Sluis; by 1460 Bruges was no longer accessible to large ships. Not based on its own fleet and dependent upon the privileges assured by the great powers, the Bruges market was threatened by the other free-trade cities. In 1488 the Emperor Maximilian proposed that foreign merchants move from Bruges to Antwerp, and from that date the great international trading centre became a secluded and illustrious provincial city.

According to similar rules the other Flemish commercial and industrial cities developed in this same period: Ghent, Louvain, Malines, Brussels, Ypres, Tournai. Ghent, which was the most important textile centre and forged a shrewd political alliance with England in the war with the French kings, became one of the largest cities in Europe with an area of 570 hectares within the thirteenth-century walls.

The German port cities of the 'Mediterranean of the north'[10] served an exclusively commercial function and were relatively small; none the less, together they managed to establish for themselves a role of considerable importance thanks to the Hanseatic political and military alliance. The initial nucleus was formed

31   Lübeck: aerial view (photo: Schonig and Co., Lübeck, SH no. 6639).

by the 1241 pact between Hamburg and Lübeck, to which were added subsequently Bremen, Rostock, Stralsund, Wismar and Lüneburg. At its peak the Hanseatic League included about ninety coastal and inland cities of various nations, including Dinant, Göttingen, Halle, Breslau (Wroclaw), Cracow, Kalmar and Reval (Tallinn).

Lübeck held a prominent position in the League and was also, from an architectural point of view, the largest and most interesting of these cities. The initial settlement at the confluence of the Rivers Trave and Wakenitz was expanded by Henry the Lion in 1173 to occupy all of the hill between the two rivers, and the city would continue to carry the mark of this original plan. Two parallel roads ran along the ridge connecting the most important civil and religious centres, while a series of perpendicular streets descended on either side conforming to the curving slopes. A series of gabled merchant houses were situated on uniform narrow and deep lots, and created a convex setting, crowned by the emerging elements of the cathedral and by the other public buildings, and given uniformity by the general use of the local red brick. The decorated façades served to publicize the merchant business conducted within these houses, where the rigid building system concentrated home, office, workshop and storage. Already entirely built up at the end of the thirteenth century, the city would maintain this constant form, with an area of 110 hectares and a population between 20,000 and 30,000.

Lübeck was one of the first of the new cities founded on the Baltic coast. Riga was founded at the beginning of the thirteenth century, Rostock in 1218, and Stralsund and Danzig (Gdansk) around 1230. The Baltic, however, had been travelled four centuries earlier by the Normans, and the Varangians, Scandinavian trader-warriors, had penetrated along the rivers of the Russian plain. In the first half of the ninth century, the legendary Rurik founded Novgorod on the Volkhov river. The situation of this huge country, with two connected river systems flowing out into the Baltic and Black Seas, allowed communication with the south, and so the famous and longed-for objective of Constantinople.

32 *Danzig: reconstruction of the city centre (from K. Gruber,* Die Gestalt der deutschen Stadt, *Munich, Callwey, 1983).*

Already in 860 an expedition had sailed down the Dnieper River and approached the Bosporus. In 880, Oleg, Rurik's successor, founded the first Russian kingdom, Kievan Rus, and in 912 a fleet of 2,000 ships arrived at Constantinople and secured a trading agreement.

The capital cities of this state – Kiev and then Suzdal from 1125 and Vladimir from 1157 – consisted of various fortified enclosures conforming to the terrain and surrounded by embankments and wooden fences. These were the outposts of the European world on the edge of the vast Asian expanse; they completed a commercial and civil circuit between the northern and southern seas and maintained relationships with the Eastern Empire as well as with the Ottonian Empire of the west. The surviving monuments – the cathedral of St Sofia in Kiev, the two churches of the *kremlin* (fortress) in Vladimir and the cathedral of Suzdal – combine the Byzantine model of the inscribed cross with Romanesque structures and ornaments in freestone.

The arrival of the Mongols interrupted this process of consolidation; between 1237 and 1240 they conquered the Russian cities and pushed as far west as Poland, destroying Breslau and Crakow in 1241. The long Mongol occupation of the thirteenth and fourteenth centuries – the period of the major development of the European medieval city – checked the growth of the cities in this area and caused Russia to develop along different lines from the rest of Europe. Only in the early eighteenth century, under Peter the Great, did Russia break out of its isolation.

Novgorod was an exception, escaping from Mongol attack in 1238 and developing in the following centuries as the principal trading centre between east and west. On the left bank of the river a large city – about 150 hectares and 20,000 inhabitants – grew up around the *kremlin*; on the opposite shore a commercial centre was established specifically equipped for both river and land traffic. Several important trade routes met here: the Great Road from Karelia to the west and the Prussian road from Riga and the Baltic, and from the east the roads from Moscow and Lake Ladoga. An imposing circle of walls was completed in 1383, enclosing the urban organism within a roundish perimeter.

The new Russian principality gained independence from the Mongols in 1380. Its capital was Moscow which, however, took on the appearance of a city only in the fifteenth and sixteenth

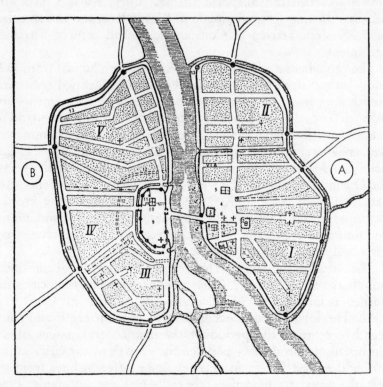

33   *Novgorod: reconstruction of the Hanseatic city (from E. Ennen,* Die europaeische Stadt des Mittelalters, *Göttingen: Vandenhoeck and Ruprecht, 1972), based on the work of Tolstoy and Nikitsky, and on K. V. Kudrashov, 'Russian Historical Atlas'. (A) Commercial side; (B) St Sophia side: (I) Slavno district; (II) Carpenters' district; (III) People's (or Potters') district; (IV) Castle-back district; (V) Nerevsky district; (1) Gothic Square, with Church of St Olaf, cemetery, meadow and landing-place; (2) Square of St Peter of the Germans; (3) Pskov Court, possibly the old court of the guild of Gotland merchants; (4) market-place; (5) Church of St John (Russian merchants); (6) Good Friday Church (Russian merchants engaged in long-distance trade); (7) Square of Prince John the Wise, with dismantled fortifications; (8) Church of St Nicholas; (9) the fortress (Djetinec); (10) Cathedral of St Sophia; (11) archbishop's castle; (12) castle moat; (13) city ramparts and turreted walls.*

centuries. Russia conquered Novgorod in 1478 and so ended the latter's role as intermediary between east and west. Russia rejected relations with Europe and, after the fall of Constantinople in 1453, considered itself to be the religious and political heir of Orthodox civilization, in opposition to that of the West – an attitude that prolonged the country's isolation from the rest of Europe.

Colonization and the New Cities

The closed city, as distinguished from the open countryside, initiated a general transformation of the territory of Europe beginning in the twelfth century. The city imported foodstuffs and raw materials and exported the products of commerce and industry. These exchanges, together with general demographic increase, required that the countryside increase production, cultivating new lands and better exploiting those already under cultivation. At the same time, the borders of Europe expanded to the east with the colonization of lands across the Elbe, and to the south with the gradual reconquest of the Arab territories in Spain. These various processes required the founding of new cities – by kings, by feudal lords, by religious orders or by the larger cities – which conformed in differing degrees with the urban models already in existence.

On a smaller scale, these new cities reproduced the municipal organization of the city-state, while remaining politically and judicially subject to an external power, whether feudal or of another city: the personal freedom of the workers was guaranteed; a local government was almost always elected by the citizens themselves; and similar organizational and formal principles were employed.

It was in this way that by the fourteenth century the tight multi-centred organization that still characterizes Europe was created. French scholars counted 130,000 bell towers dotting the continent from the Mediterranean to the Arctic Sea. Often close together – 5–10 km apart in the most populous areas – the corresponding settlements were none the less differentiated by countless variations of language, architecture, habits and ideas. These differences determined the confrontations that fuelled the initiatives and dynamism of Europe as it prepared to confront the rest of the world.

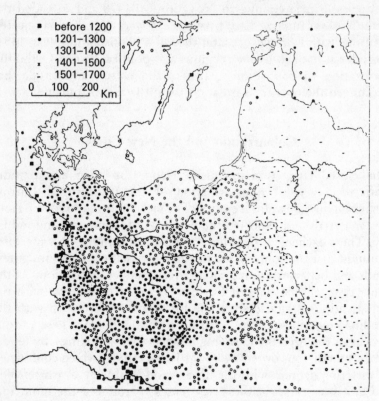

34   European colonization beyond the Elbe (from C. T. Smith, An Historical Atlas of Western Europe before 1800, *1967).*

The small cities founded on new sites reveal the ability to conceptualize and create a planned urban organism. Their shape was determined at the moment of founding and often remained unchanged through time. The founder of each was also the owner of the terrain on which it sat and so could rationally plan the design of the city in all its particulars: roads, squares, fortifications, and also the subdivision into lots for the inhabitants, a process undertaken with reference to known and shared building models.

The new cities came in every possible form, forms that past scholars have attempted to classify without finding a consistent explanation for the choice of one type or another. The circumstances to be taken into consideration, even for a single initial decision, are almost innumerable: the nature of the terrain, local traditions or foreign influences, sacred and profane symbolism, unprejudiced adherence to functional and economic necessities; and in a given situation any one of these might become determinant.

The distinction we normally make between the planning of a city and the planning of a building was vague. Many buildings were gradually modified in time like the cities themselves, and many cities were conceived from the start like the buildings, and often by the same designers: Arnolfo, for example, who designed the Florentine colonies of San Giovanni Valdarno and Castelfranco di Sopra. The planning of a city seems to have been a special case of the general ability to manage visible forms in time. In fact, the late twelfth-century change in the planning of buildings applied to the new cities as well. The first of these – prior to Montauban (founded in 1144) – had irregular and non-repeatable designs. Subsequently, and contemporary to the spread of the Gothic style, an orthogonal plan adaptable to many different situations became common; it often developed into a perfectly regular weft, like the Hippodamian plans of the ancient Roman colonial cities.[11]

The newly founded cities of the thirteenth century – the *bastides* of southern France promoted by the two combatants of the Hundred Years War (Aigues Mortes 1246, Sainte-Foy-la-Grande 1255, Monségur 1263, Villeneuve-sur-Lot 1264, Beaumont 1272, Montpazier 1284), the English 'new towns' (Liverpool 1207, New Salisbury 1219, Flint 1272, New Winchelsea 1292), the Frankish cities of northern Italy (Orzinuovi 1198, Cittadella 1210, Gattinara 1242, Cherasco 1248, Massalombarda 1251, Montagnana 1257) and of central Italy (Buonconvento 1242, Pietrasanta 1255, San Giovanni Valdarno 1296), the *poblaciones* of southern Spain (Briviesca 1208, Villacarillo 1212, Salvatierra 1256, Villareal 1272), and the cities founded by the Teutonic order in the east (Torun 1231, Königsberg 1255) and by Charles d'Anjou in the south (L'Aquila 1266, Cittaducale 1309) – were on a technical and visual par with the planned enlargements of two Italian cities (Brescia 1235 and Florence 1293) in which there already existed a basic Roman grid. In these latter two cities, modifications conformed to the restrictions of the existing organism and were composed of large ordered rectilinear elements: the stretches of the polygonal city walls, roads of constant width like Via Matteotti in Brescia and Via Maggio in

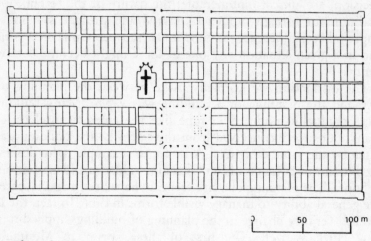

0   50   100 m

35   Plan of Montpazier, founded in 1284.

Florence, and the regular parallel arrangement of the bordering lots.

In these urban designs, as in those of the cathedrals, mental reference is made to the three orthogonal dimensions, and while these are of necessity occasionally violated, they none the less ensure continuity of concept and largely normalize the unity of the distributive structure. Taking this point of view, Gothic design can be understood as a method for the organization of space, any space, according to a universal framework expandable to virtually any scale (even though the Renaissance concept of perspective is still lacking). One takes possession of inhabitable space and forces it through an intellectual grating that extends over the entire dimensional gamut.

From another point of view, the architectural comparison does not stand up, for the age in which the new cities were founded was relatively short, from the mid-twelfth to the mid-fourteenth century. The process was interrupted by the demographic and economic crises following the Black Death of 1348, which halted the construction of new cities in Europe and permitted the execution of only a few refoundings in the peripheral areas of the south and east. During the fourteenth and fifteenth centuries the art of designing a building changed, and benefited from a series of

36   Salisbury: aerial view, showing the cathedral (photo: Aerofilms Ltd, no. A 58294).

theoretical and practical considerations, while at the same time the art of designing a city fell into disuse and was forgotten before it could be given theoretical treatment in plans and books.

Documentation does exist of a 1297 colloquium called by Edward I of England at Harwich with representatives from twenty cities of his kingdom for the purpose of discussing the best methods for designing and governing the new cities.[12] Concentration focused on the contemporary experiments: 120 cities had been founded in France and the French continental possessions, and seventy more would follow in the first half of the fourteenth century. It provides a rare written testimony from the period when the new cities were being founded and reveals the lack of interest in a general theoretical treatment. Subsequently there is only the treatise of Eximenics, written in Spain in the late fourteenth century when the practical experiences of city building were nearly forgotten and the argument could be restricted to the scientific and philosophical sphere. European culture was ill-equipped, from this point of view, just as it prepared to expand to a global scale. We shall return to this point below.

The Medieval Urban Heritage

The formation of the European city, which we can identify today as a cycle between the economic and demographic revival of the eleventh century and the recession of the fourteenth, marked at the time an adventurous leap into the unknown future. Both those, like Dante, who lamented the city 'within the ancient circle of walls' and identified that of the present day with 'new people and quick profits', and the other travellers and chroniclers, who instead described this novelty with admiration and wonder, signalled in different ways the impact of an unexpected and surprising development. A still evident aspect of the European identity emerged out of these contrasting judgements: a sense of possession and of belonging, an emotional link which would endure long into the future.

The relationship between the European cities and those of the ancient world was overturned. Constantinople (after its conquest by crusaders in 1204), Cordoba (after the reconquest of 1236), Baghdad (after the Mongol invasion of 1258) and Palermo (after the siege by Charles of Anjou in 1266) were decadent and ruined cities; while the many European centres were enjoying rapid growth and were conceived according to the greater dimensions planned for them. Between 1274 and 1291 Marco Polo visited China and the immense cities of the Yuan Empire, which far exceeded the measure of European cities, and yet he compared them as equals to Venice and other European cities. On the eve of confrontation with the rest of the world, the cities of the new Europe had reached global urban standards.

The urbanization of Europe between 1050 and 1350 is the decisive event in our story: a canvas of many differentiated centres was created, and it is still on this canvas that the present-day network of settlements in which we live is largely drawn. A good portion of the medieval centres survive today as local administrative units (independently in France in the 32,000 *communes*, combined in Italy in the 8,000 *comuni*), characterized by limited but not artificial autonomy and a real and living role in popular customs and imagination.

The urban settings created in the Middle Ages would continue to exert a strong influence on cities which subsequently multiplied in size many times. The very notion of the city as an individual and in some ways living being, immune from the recent national and supranational institutional forms, derives from this heritage. We feel that we belong to our city and characterize ourselves as Parisian, Londoner, Venetian, or even identify with the particular quarter to which we are bound. This is not a limiting characterization, but in a certain sense expansive for the richness of human experience concentrated in a particular place. The smallness of these immediate allegiances does not separate us from the world but mysteriously aids us to enter into the great horizons of our age – Europe, the global community – overcoming the more recent boundaries of national states. The correspondence between image and sentiment that we notice in these boundaries conditions all our experiences of community life.

Many general theoretical discussions of the city are based on an idealized conception of the creative medieval period – in 1925 Robert E. Park wrote: 'The city is . . . a state of mind, a body of customs and traditions, and of the organized attitudes and sentiments that inhere in these customs and are transmitted with this tradition.'[13] – yet only a renewed awareness of the historical origin of the city can correct the note of arrogance that accompanies these judgements and so derive an objective contribution to a new global culture.

3

The Perfecting of the Urban Environment

Stabilization and the Last Urban Expansions of the Fourteenth Century

The great economic depression that lasted from the first third of the fourteenth century to the middle of the fifteenth brought European urban development to a halt. Demographic expansion ceased as well (or was reversed), particularly after the plague of 1347–8. Florence lost perhaps three-quarters of the 90,000 inhabitants that it had at the beginning of the century and failed to exceed 70,000 in the following century. Building ceased, and the city did not manage to fill out the remaining area within the most recent circle of walls. Siena, Ghent, Cologne and many other large European cities suffered similar fates. The prices of necessary agricultural products declined, while wages and the prices of other goods rose in a situation of labour scarcity. In addition to difficulties and disequilibria, this combination led to the stimulation of specialized industry and commerce, improved communications (in 1338 the first carriage-passable road over the Alps was opened, from Chur to Chiavenna; at the end of the fourteenth century a regular postal service was established between Venice and Bruges), and progress in the area of finance (double entry bookkeeping was spread by the Genoese in the following century; the exchange banks of Barcelona (1401) and Valencia (1407) and the Casa di San Giorgio in Genoa (1408) were modelled after those of the Rialto in Venice; the first merchants' bargaining centre was

founded in the mid-fifteenth century by the Van der Beurs family).
Technological progress did not cease, and this period produced a
number of important inventions: canal locks and dredgers, hydraulic bellows, the rod-and-crank system, spring-operated clocks
and clocks sounding the hours. These were documented in the
early fifteenth-century treaties of Kyeser, an anonymous Hussite
War engineer and Giovanni da Fontana.[1]

Economic vicissitudes exacerbated social conflicts and the revolts of the lower classes (the artisans of Nuremberg in 1348, the
Ciompi of Florence in 1378, the Flemish textile workers in 1379,
the *tuchins* of Languedoc in 1380, the English Mile's End peasants
in 1381, and the people of Paris in 1382) were resolved to the
advantage of those already holding power, the seignory or the
national kingdoms. The latter groups reacted by limiting civil
liberties, and the cities, though maintaining importance, passed
into guardianship.[2]

At the same time, the universal institutions of the Middle Ages
were losing ground as supranational authorities were drawn into
local conflicts: the papacy was in France from 1309 to 1378, and
the Holy Roman Empire identified with the German dynastic
kingdoms. Cultural organization diversified; many new universities were founded in various countries, some even of a national
character; and the general nominalist orientation of the period
encouraged broad confrontations of interpretation and investigation.

Only in a few cases did these circumstances stimulate the further
development of existing cities in the latter half of the fourteenth
century: Avignon as the new papal seat, Prague as the imperial
capital of Charles IV (1354–78), and Nuremberg as the hub of land
communication for central Europe and as a metallurgical centre of
international scale. These are the few cases, and all the more
interesting for their rarity, of expansion in a phase of general urban
stagnation at the end of the great medieval period.

Avignon was already a medium-sized city – about 15,000 inhabitants – when Clement V decided to move his court there. The
economic means of the papacy were limited, and eight different
popes succeeded one another during the seventy years that it
remained in Avignon. Urban development, as a result, was slow
and took place in several phases: the transformation (and therefore
expansion) of the bishop's palace into a papal residence (1335 and

37   Avignon (sixteenth-century map).

1345), the work on the bridge over the Rhône , the new circle of walls (1355–70), and the peripheral forts of Saint-André and Sorgues. At mid-century the population of Avignon came to about 35,000, but this number was halved after the plague of 1348. The second thoughts and economic difficulties that slowed the development of Avignon did not disturb the compactness of this lovely Provençal setting, built of the local freestone and according to a severe Gothic discipline. On the other hand, the splendid interiors – which can be glimpsed in the surviving bits of Simone Martini frescos – have been all but destroyed in the past two centuries, and the last unfortunate restorations of the Papal Palace did the rest. None the less, in the uniform golden light that bathes all elements of the local landscape, the setting produced by this historic adventure sits as a solemnly concluded project.

Charles IV of Luxemburg, king of Bohemia from 1341, worked constantly at the development of Prague. In 1344 he promoted the establishment of an archbishopric there and in 1348 founded the first university of eastern Europe. In that same year he began the 'new city' which expanded the urban area by over 200 hectares and formed, together with the two existing settlements (the 'old city' of 1232 and the 1257 German colony of Malà Strana), a great city of European scale: about 320 hectares and 50,000 inhabitants.

In 1355, when Charles was elected emperor, Prague became the capital of the Holy Roman Empire and a massive programme of public works was begun, including the monumental bridge of twenty-four arches across the Vltava (1357) and the vast squares of the new city. The centre of the old city received a new architectural face with the municipal tower of 1364 and the Tyn church of 1365. The castle (Hrad) on the hill was crowned by a huge Gothic cathedral, finished only in 1392; at its base the new quarter along the right bank of the river began to take shape in 1360. This fourteenth-century assemblage, unique in Europe for its size, was able to sustain the subsequent late Gothic, Renaissance and Baroque additions that give Prague its composite physiognomy. Yet under the Classical veneer of the long castle wall facing the valley, it is not difficult to discern the austere and repetitive medieval model. Miraculously, this city has survived virtually unscathed to the present day and gives us a concrete idea of the large-scale inventive ability of the late Gothic period, so rarely realized.

Nuremberg also stands out in this period, but is a product of the municipal-industrial sphere rather than of the courts. Only in 1320 did the two settlements founded by Henry III and Frederick I on either side of the River Pegnitz – and at the point of intersection for the communication routes linking Bavaria, Franconia, Swabia and Bohemia – join together to form a single city within an almost circular ring of walls astride the river. Settlements rapidly sprang up in the level areas to the south and east, and in the second half of the fourteenth century the walls were expanded to include these in the city. This new ring was one of the most elaborate military constructions of the time: two parallel walls reinforced with towers and surrounded by a large external moat. The city filled an area of 160 hectares and numbered 20,000 inhabitants.

The city centre was rebuilt from 1348. The oldest nucleus of houses was torn down to free space for the market square, and the most important public structures were built: the Church of St Mary (1355), the new choir of the Church of St Sebald (1361), the famous fountain (1385), and the new choir of the Church of St Lorenz (1439) and the case for the Holy Sacrament within it; these

38   Nuremberg (engraving dated 1493).

are among the most important monuments of German late Gothic. The city hall was begun in the fourteenth century and enlarged in the sixteenth and seventeenth centuries, but with a singular continuity of style.

From this circumscribed and compact nucleus, Nuremberg long held economic and cultural sway over a large area of central Europe. The city government was controlled by the great merchant families and later by the bankers, like the Welsers, who operated on a global scale. The great German sculptors – Veit Stoss, the Vischer family – worked here as well as Albrecht Dürer, Hans Sachs and the early sixteenth-century typographers and cartographers. As a result of the destruction of the Second World War and the subsequent hasty rebuilding of the old centre the traditional setting has essentially been lost; only the carefully restored monuments remain.

Representation of the Stabilized City

The developments in these three cities are exceptions in an age of stabilization and withdrawal which generally witnessed a decline of the city-building project that had characterized the previous phase. Whatever size and shape happened to have been achieved in the late thirteenth and early fourteenth centuries became definitive, and both the habits and imagination of individuals and groups adapted to these. The strong push for stylistic uniformity, which had previously produced the unobjectionable new cities described above, generally translated into a more careful reading of the existing setting and its celebration and perfection in literary representations, painted and sculpted images and a few limited building operations.

The great writers of the age opened their eyes to the world around them. Petrarch penned the first realistic and first-hand descriptions of the cities he visited. In 1358 he visited Genoa and wrote: 'You will see a regal city backed up against a steep range of hills, proud of its population and its walls; its appearance alone declares it master of the sea.'³ In 1356 he was in Prague and recorded his appreciation both of the city's beauty and of the emperor's humanity. He spent many years in Avignon – between 1330 and 1340 and again after 1347 – and provided in his writings the best portrait we have of the papal capital. His curiosity led him to climb Mont Ventoux in 1336 'urged on by the simple desire to see a place famous for its great height', and he wrote the first objective account of a landscape viewed from above. In that same year he made his first trip to Rome and emotionally recounted the visual setting of the great city in ruins. In the *Seniles* letters he described the Venetian celebrations of 1363 held in 'that piazza, probably unmatched in all the world, lying in front of the gold and marble façade of the basilica. The great piazza, the basilica itself, the towers, rooftops, porticoes, windows and all possible observation points were filled with spectators. Nothing gave people more pleasure than to see joy in the faces of all.'⁴ No one had observed the great European scenario, its cities and their settings, so precisely and with so much interest.

The humanist writers of the two following generations – including Enea Silvio Piccolomini, 'eager to see much' both before and after his election to the papal throne in 1458 – shifted freely between descriptions of physical and psychological landscapes.⁵ They created the genre of city *laudationes*, written for polemical, political and rhetorical purposes, but often revealing a rich understanding of the character and individuality the city described: the writings of Salutati and Loschi in the dispute between republican Florence and Milan under Gian Galeazzo Visconti, Bruni's *laudatio* of Florence and an anonymous *laudatio* of Genoa in 1430.

Painting, revived by the great Florentine and Sienese masters of the late thirteenth century, was another tool for representing the world spectacle, able to reflect and order the entire universe of natural and artificial forms. The existing urban settings found descriptive and normative confirmation in illuminated manuscripts, painted on wooden panels or as frescos on the interior walls of buildings; in these various media the entire range of theological, philosophical, ceremonial and worldly activities was silently recorded and ordered in accordance with the dictates of visual coherence. Toward the middle of the fourteenth century the first non-symbolic city maps appeared, like that of Venice already described, as well as the first landscapes not linked to a particular tale or event, like the Sienese panels of the Lorenzetti school. The relationship between word and image – to which Huizinga devotes two chapters of his *Waning of the Middle Ages*[6] – was overturned in this period, and it was this visual culture of the early fifteenth century that initiated the stylistic revolution of the Renaissance.

The final moments of the urban development described in the preceding section was dominated by the presence of artists, painters and sculptors: Giotto, Arnolfo and Ghiberti in Florence; Duccio, Simone Martini and the Lorenzettis in Siena; Jan van Eyck and Memling in Bruges; Stoss and Dürer in Nuremberg. Contemporaries were perfectly aware of the importance of their work; one need only recall the 1311 procession which transported the *Maestà* of Duccio from the painter's studio to the great altar of the cathedral. And though until the end of the fifteenth century painters and sculptors worked within the guild system (in Florence, painters were included with the physicians and herbalists who provided their colours; sculptors in stone were included with stonemasons and carpenters; and sculptors in metal and goldsmiths with silk workers, a category including the various workers in luxury goods), their abilities were not perceived as limited to a particular sort of work or material, but instead entailed a general mastery of the visible form, an ability which enabled them to give advice also in the fields of architecture and urban design. As already mentioned, Arnolfo designed the new urban system of Florence in the last decade of the thirteenth century; and Giotto designed the campanile in 1334.

It is from these high-level consultants, rather than from those responsible for the actual constructions of the previous period, that we can trace the experience of the Renaissance artist and the stylistic revolution that in the following two centuries everywhere replaced the world of forms developed before.

The New Artistic Culture

It was the perfecting of the urban organism that above all characterized the European city in this period: the completion and ornamentation of the principal buildings, the organization of public spaces, and the construction of new public and private buildings. Aesthetic considerations, including questions of durability, convenience and visual evenness, were behind many of these operations and found expression in administrative regulations as well: the Florentine statutes of 1415, for example, dealt at length with these questions. Stone or brick pavement, previously found only in a few cities or important places (Lübeck, Piazza San Marco in Venice), spread to many other areas. The use of certain materials and typical stylistic elements was in some cases prescribed as a sign of urban individuality. Design questions for an important building, like the cathedral of Florence begun at the end of the thirteenth century or that of Milan begun a century later, were debated one by one with great determination: the 1367 competition for the type of pillar to be used in Santa Maria del Fiore (Florence), for example. Because of the independence and conceptual equality of each detail in a Gothic construction, this sort of debate eventually led to an impossible waste of energy. Occasionally this method led to pleasing results, like the façade of the cathedral in Orvieto, slowly built between 1310 and 1425, or the Reliquary of the Corporal inside the same building produced by Ugolino di Vieri and his partners in 1337–8, structures suspended in a precarious balance and forming a jealously isolated universe closed off to further development. More often the single elements acquired undue complication, piling up monotonously, as in the courtly literature or the polyphonic music of the period.

Change occurred in an exceedingly narrow space and time: in Florence between the competition for the dome of the cathedral (1418) and the year of its completion (1436). Artists (Ghiberti, Brunelleschi, Donatello, Paolo Uccello, Nanni di Banco,

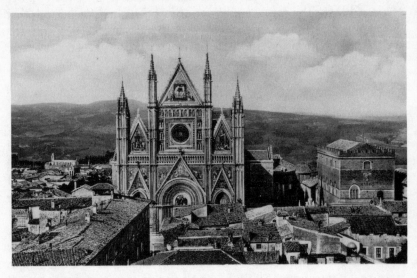

39   *Orvieto: the cathedral façade rising above the surrounding rooftops (photo: Benevolo).*

Masaccio), authors (Salutati, Bruni), and scientists (Toscanelli, Pelicani) together questioned the roles of traditional culture. As far as we can tell, the important choices were made by a single individual, Filippo Brunelleschi, and applied to both architecture and the figurative arts.

The move to understand and control the world of visible forms received a scientific and definitive response: linear perspective, which established a precise correspondence between artistic, painted or sculpted representations and the three-dimensional forms of the objects represented. Perspective ordered the world of images according to a specific hierarchy: first proportional relationships and then measurements and physical characteristics, texture and colour. From this hierarchy were derived generally applicable rules of design for architecture and for the cityscape. In order to apply this method on a large scale, the elements making up the perspective canvas needed fixed and recognizable forms. Their easy identification allowed quick recognition of this canvas, which varied according to functional and representative requirements, and also established a frame of reference for the evaluation of particulars: the specific modifications of fixed elements, within the limits of recognizability, and of accessory elements as well. Paintings and sculptures were among these elements but possessed their own visual organization independent of the context, within which one found virtually the entire world spectacle including its landscape, architecture and human characters. The normalized elemental (as opposed to general) models derived from Classical antiquity and had been present to some degree throughout the Middle Ages, especially in Tuscany. Now, however, they were copied first-hand from the ancient monuments in order to fill this new intellectual function.

Both components of the new method – the geometric theory of perspective and reference to the normalized elements of antiquity – possessed a previous history. The decisive step, however, was their unexpected and fertile combination. It was not a coincidence that this methodological shift occurred on the occasion of the building of the dome which completed, after more than a century, the cathedral of Florence. In Leonardo Bruni's *laudatio* Florence is

40   *Florence: Brunelleschi's dome as part of the city panorama (photo: Benevolo).*

represented by a series of concentric circles at the centre of which stands symbolically the Palazzo della Signoria; this same imagery was employed in Dati's *Istoria* of 1422–4. The late fourteenth-century decision to elevate the dome by construction of the tambour served to create the visual, as opposed to the symbolic, centre of the urban organism. Brunelleschi transformed this intention into a precise image by constructing a grandiose dome, visible from great distances and characterized by its frame of eight curved members directed toward every spatial angle. These members come together in the pivot of the lantern, whose classical frame was enlarged to absorb the full force of the sunlight. Symbol of the new architecture, Brunelleschi's dome dominated the centre of the cityscape, and brought the cathedral, designed in the late thirteenth century, to a definitive and forward-looking conclusion. The flower (*fiore*) metaphor became a visible design of which the dome formed the centre and the surrounding, approximately circular, city walls the outer edge of the petals. Florence was in fact represented in this way in the first perspective view of 1472. Both Bruni and Landino in the preface to the *Divine Comedy* describe Florence as the true heir to Rome, guardian of ancient and Christian virtues. In 1954 Chastel published the illuminated initial of a codex of *The City of God* in which the holy city contemplated

41   *Florence: view dating from 1472 (engraved by C. Duchet, c. 1580).*

by St Augustine is in fact Florence, its towers and campanili dominated by the cupola of Brunelleschi.[7]

The other Florentine works of Brunelleschi in which he experimented with the new design method – the Ospedale degli Innocenti, the old sacristy in San Lorenzo, the Palazzo di Parte Guelfa, the rebuilt Churches of San Lorenzo and Santo Spirito, the Pazzi Chapel in Santa Croce, and the Rotonda degli Angeli, all located at key points of the by now stabilized city – almost inevitably encountered difficulties and were completed after his death (1446) and with significant alterations. None the less, this collection of structures, built in response to the needs and difficulties of early fifteenth-century Florence, subsequently served as the required model for Italian and European architectural experimentation. In a century and a half it entirely replaced the previous traditions with a repertory that remained universally valid and binding until the nineteenth century. In making this choice, European culture distanced itself from the Mediterranean lingua franca; appropriated the Graeco-Roman heritage, the basis of other Western traditions as well (Byzantine, Arab, Coptic, Russian); and forged with it a relationship that overarched the course of time. It was a relationship founded on intellectual calculation and the reclaiming of ancient sources. The European experience acquired new authority and stability, the consequences of which revealed themselves in the following centuries.

The Renewal of Urban Planning in Italy

The application of the new method on an urban scale was problematic from the beginning. The European urban system was essentially complete, and it would be some time before further modification was either obviously needed or easily afforded. On the other hand, this cultural transition, which brought into play and emphasized the legacy of the past, eased somewhat the difficulties inherent in change. In the case of Florence, the urban framework established in the time of Arnolfo a century and a half before was never challenged. The new architectural methods served in fact to preserve and perfect the existing design which risked submersion under a confusion of unnecessary details.

Contradictions did arise in the relations between artists, patrons and society. The great medieval projects were possible because they depended upon collective efforts, according to the technical and administrative arrangements of the city-states. Nor was this procedure immediately abandoned. It is worthy of note that work on the dome, far and away the most costly and involved of Brunelleschi's projects, was also that completed most expeditiously; it was financed by the Lana (wool) guild and contracted according to the usual series of competitions and approvals. The inventors of the new artistic culture were part of this world – Brunelleschi was prior of San Giovanni in 1425 – but also achieved a degree of autonomy from the collective by means of the new patronage of the seignorial familes – for Brunelleschi the Medici and the Pazzi. However, as revealed by the examples of San Lorenzo and the Santa Croce chapel, these families did not yet possess proportionate means.

The artists of the following generation freed themselves from the civic collective and moved willingly into the court milieu of the princes (who shared their cultural education). Political calm and the economic boom of the late fifteenth century generated new needs as well as the resources necessary to satisfy them. However, the personal initiative of the princes, fickle and authoritarian, was appropriate to individual architectural projects, not the complexities of urban planning. At the end of the fifteenth century as at the beginning, though for an entirely different reason, modification of the urban organism remained impossible. There was, however, a middle period during which the political and economic situation had changed sufficiently, the collective mechanisms were not excessively weakened, and luck had it that patrons and artists managed an extended collaboration; and it was in this period that the gap between cultural ideals and concrete accomplishments lessened and the significant transformation of several medium-sized Italian cities was achieved.

The Theoretical Mediation of Alberti

In 1434, when the Florentine cultural transformation was nearly complete, the thirty-year-old Leon Battista Alberti arrived in the Tuscan capital. These were the first years of Medici rule; Brunelleschi was about to finish his dome and almost all of his projects were under way; Ghiberti was working on the third door of the Baptistery; Paolo Uccello and Donatello had returned to the city; and the artists of the new generation – Michelozzo, Fra Angelico, Filippo Lippi, Rossellino, Luca della Robbia – took as their starting point the recent discoveries. The young author entered into the world of visual arts, attempting to give theoretical expression to the recent developments in his treatises on sculpture and painting, around 1436, and again later in that on architecture, dedicated to Pope Nicholas II in 1452. His purpose, however, was not simply theoretical. Using the universal tool of humanist culture, the written word, and taking into consideration with equal seriousness all concrete developments, Alberti attempted to bring order to those proposals already advanced in an attempt to make their practical application both more general and more secure. Alberti's work influenced much of Italian urban transformation from the 1440s to the 1470s, and his discussion of architecture is filled with references to the estimates and budgets of these projects.

In the 1452 treatise Alberti records all the ambiguities of the new culture as it confronted the problem of the city: architecture is a complex operation and includes both planning (*lineamenta*) and construction (*structura*). Its domain potentially includes all the various building scales according to the enumeration of successive 'parts': *regio, area, partitio, paries, tectum, apertio*. In the Italian edition Cosimo Bartoli translated *structura* with *muramenti* or walling, emphasizing Alberti's intention to reduce all raised structures to the concept of the wall. The architectural categories on which the perspective analysis of a building depended were derived from a wall 'open and split in many places' and were themselves described as architectural 'ornaments'. Here was a way to mediate between medieval practices and the new artistic culture; it would serve as a guide (and make possible) the urban transformations of the succeeding decades: Pienza, Urbino, Mantua, Ferrara, Rome, Naples.

Book 4, dedicated to 'all the works in their totality', that is to the city, does not propose a design scheme on this scale, but rather considers the city as the setting in which the various projects are combined, fixed in time and dominated by the permanent factors of terrain and climate. It could not have a regular form, like that required of buildings, but 'varied with the variation of places'. Describing the separate elements of the city in book 8 – streets,

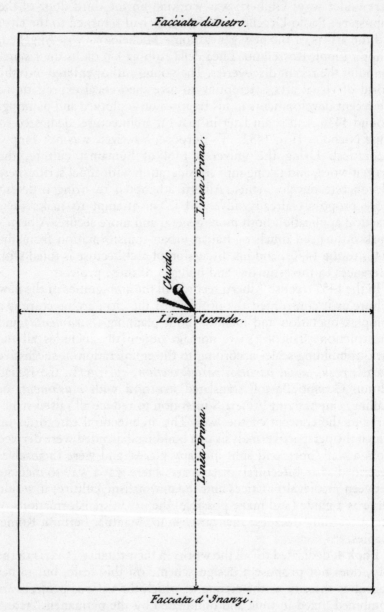

42   *The principle of symmetry (illustration from Alberti's treatise* De re aedificatoria, *ed. Leoni, 1755).*

squares – Alberti prudently oscillates between regularity and irregularity, focusing attention on concrete possibilities.

His writings are marked by a particular personal touch that has always made them convincing. His direct experiences became norms and so weighed on subsequent developments of theory and practice. The methodological leap from urban planning to that of single structures broke the continuity of the late Gothic tradition and would remain a lasting characteristic of European culture, still felt today.

The two categories of conceptual references, spatial and environmental, are theoretically and historically heterogeneous. Yet it is just their mediation that made possible the actions taken in that particular historical context. Inherent contradictions were of minor importance in the smaller cities where transformation was more coherent, but became decisive in the larger ones where Renaissance modifications upset the existing balance without re-establishing a new one.

The Small Cities of the Renaissance Princes: Pienza, Urbino, Ferrara

The combination of a sufficiently long period of enlightened patronage – Pius II in Pienza between 1459 and 1464, Federico di Montefeltro in Urbino between 1447 and 1482, Ludovico III Gonzaga in Mantua between 1444 and 1478, Borso and Ercole I d'Este in Ferrara between 1450 and 1505 – adequate economic and organizational resources, and an abundance of intellectual support – Alberti himself, Rossellino, Piero della Francesca, Fancelli, Mantegna, Rossetti and the Ferrarese painters – made possible the adaptation of several small and medium-sized cities to the new cultural norms. In these, theoretical contradictions were overcome and a qualitative leap for the entire organism was accomplished by means of a series of architectural devices.

On a trip to Mantua in 1459 Pius II visited his native village of Corsignano together with Alberti and decided both to rebuild it and to give it the new name of Pienza. The rapid and successful completion of this project owes much to its clearly limited scope, as set out in the bull of 1462: 'Build an entirely new and magnificent church, together with an illustrious palazzo, where the paternal home stands, and several other structures.' The new

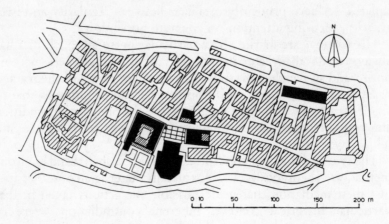

43   Map of Pienza (Pius II's buildings in black).

buildings were concentrated in the centre of the village, where the main street bends following the crest of the hill; within their orthogonal arrangement there opened on this curve a trapezium-shaped piazza at the back of which stood the church framed between two openings to the external space of the valley below.

The monumental structures, built of the local stone, stand out from the others for their regularity and obvious importance. None the less, they conform to the complex of pre-existing structures. In the piazza, paved in large squares, regularity and irregularity offset one another with extreme clarity. In the church, designed by Rossellino who took as his model the German *Hallenkirchen* he had encountered on his travels, Pius placed the paintings he had expressly commissioned from the Sienese painters of the day (Sano di Pietro, Vecchietta, Giovanni di Paolo and Matteo di Giovanni) isolating them after the fashion of Alberti against the starkness of the walls and so intimating the excommunication that awaited anyone who in future attempted the slightest modification. The Piccolomini Palace has a panoramic loggia which occupies the entire southern façade and opens out upon a view of Amiata, that 'mountain beautiful to look upon'. This dream of the humanist pope, given concrete form, is an unsurpassed example of the intelligent transition from project to execution that was among the major concerns of fifteenth-century thought. It has come to us intact as an example of the victory of *virtus* over *fortuna*.

44   *A street in Pienza (photo: Benevolo).*

Urbino too was the product of a happy, and longer-lasting, coming together of circumstances. Duke Federico di Montefeltro transformed his city with the same spirit of prudence and moderation he employed in his military and diplomatic dealings, and thanks to the considerable sums earned as *Condottiere* (captain of

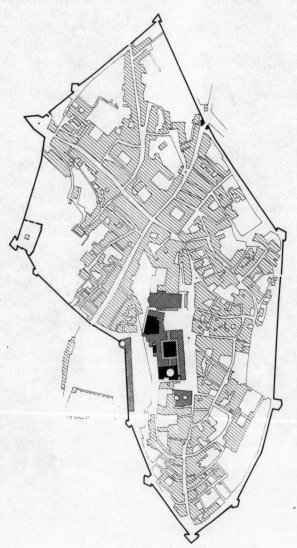

45   Map of Urbino (the Ducal Palace and cathedral shaded).

mercenaries) of Venice and the Italian League. In his small Apennine capital he brought together an exceptional group of Italian and European personages – Piero della Francesca, Luciano Laurana, Francesco di Giorgio, Justus of Ghent, Pedro Berruguete and Paul von Middelburg – and assembled with the collaboration of Vespasiano da Bisticci the most important library of the period, later added to the Vatican collection.

The Ducal Palace is deftly inserted into the urban organism, without interfering with the existing fabric of structures. Its positioning allowed the opening up of the Piazza Ducale on the side toward the hill, while on that toward the valley, the entire cliff down to Mercatale was redesigned with a collection of loggias and suspended gardens. This great structure fills up two rows of lots according to the original Roman and medieval pattern, and takes over as its monumental axis the intermediate passageway which crosses the Court of Honour and the Court of Pasquino and was intended to lead to the round funeral temple (never built). All the 'walling' conforms to the materials and dimensions of the city framework, with the exaggerated exception of the peaks of the two towers. Architectural 'ornaments' serve to give a noble quality to certain special elements of the palace and the urban organism, without ever straining the environmental and structural context.

46   *Urbino from the south-west (photo: Benevolo).*

The outstanding quality of the detail reflects the study of form found in Piero della Francesca's painting. For the duke, Piero painted a *Flagellation*, the twin portraits of Federico and his wife (Battista Sforza), and the Montefeltro altarpiece, capturing unforgettably the image of the court of Urbino and its master. The controlled use of traditional idiom in combination with imported and invented features suggests that the professional skill of the artists was directed by a fine intellect, perhaps Federico himself, and that this was the unseen but decisive unifying influence that gave coherence to the city plan.

The finest works of the visual arts were placed in the duke's study (on which Baccio Pontelli, Giuliano da Maiano, Justus of Ghent, Pedro Berruguete, Sandro Botticelli, Francesco di Giorgio, and perhaps Bramante the younger all worked), located between the internal rooms and the upper external loggia that opens on to the surrounding countryside.

This high level of activity declined immediately after the duke's death. The riches of the palace were partially dispersed, including even Piero della Francesca's twin portraits of the duke and duchess, which eventually arrived in Florence after transfer to the Vatican in 1631. But the splendid urban setting, built to the scale of a community that would return to secondary status, remains protected in the Apennine landscape and still today gives us an idea of the international city built in a brief space of time by Federico.

Ferrara was already one of the most important Italian courts in the fourteenth century, visited by Petrarch and site of a university. Leonello d'Este, himself a man of letters, was host to Jacopo Bellini, Alberti, Pisanello, Mantegna, Peter and Roger van der Weyden, and in 1436 Guarino Veronese who founded his famous school. Boiardo, and later Ariosto and Tasso, celebrated the city of the d'Este, 'capital of modern poetry' according to Chastel and so one of the most important locations for the Italian Renaissance.[8]

This medieval city, stretched in a fish bone pattern along the bank of a branch of the Po, was expanded in 1451 by Borso d'Este to include the high-water area of Sant' Antonio, and again in 1492 by Ercole I, who took over the opposite bank and enclosed a vast grid of large streets within a circle of walls. This effort, however, started late, and subsequent adversity prevented the completed building of the entire space. Ferrara became a double city. The older, densely constructed zone was separated by the earlier walls

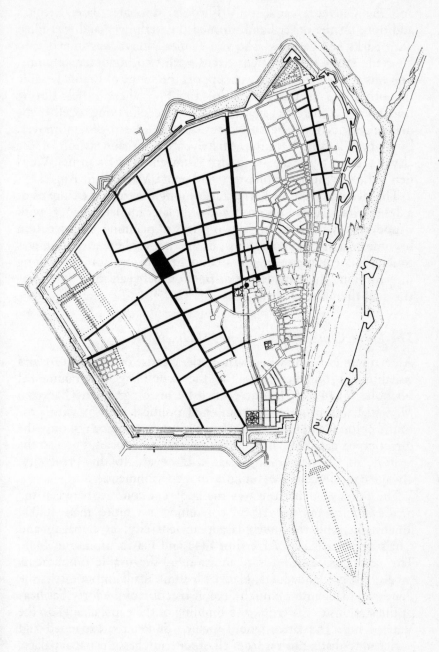

47   Map of Ferrara in the sixteenth century, showing the additions of 1451 and 1492.

and the Giovecca canal, only filled in at a later date. Ercole's addition, on the other hand, formed the periphery and was filled with parks and gardens. The vast Piazza Nuova was intended to have the shape of an ancient circus with two honorary columns; one was erected at its centre to support the statue of Ercole I, while the other lies at the bottom of the Po, where it fell during transport. Yet this open space did not succeed in tying together the main elements of the Belfiore fortifications – destroyed, moreover, by Pope Clement VIII immediately after the annexation of the city, together with the frescos of Tura and Peter van der Weyden – the Carthusian monastery and Santa Maria degli Angeli.

The two additions to Ferrara are among the earliest examples of a design first planned on paper and only later implemented, as with a modern city plan. Alberti's two stages of planning and execution become two distinct operations; in the first of these execution was timely and complete; in the second the process suffered a long interruption which made the distinction between the two operations all the more evident.

The Large Cities: Rome, Venice, Milan, Naples

Alberti was in Rome while writing the treatise on architecture and collaborated on the plans for the rebuilding programme of Nicholas V (1447–55). As recorded by his biographer, Gianozzo Manetti,[9] this programme combined political realism with profound cultural and religious motivation; it determined not only the direction of papal building in the following centuries, but also the attitude of the new ruling class with regard to this great city, always considered the defining urban environment.

The point of departure was the apparent contrast between the medieval city on the Tiber, containing no more than 40,000 inhabitants, and the much larger ancient city, both pagan and Christian, recalled by Alberti in 1443 and Flavio Biondo in 1446. The new plan called for restoration of the usable monuments (walls, bridges, aqueducts, Hadrian's tomb made into a castle, the Pantheon made into a church), reconstruction of the forty basilicas of the stations of the cross, and building of the papal citadel on the Vatican hill. The latter would include St Peter's, expanded and enriched to distinguish it from all other churches, the papal palace, a theatre, a library, a park, a botanical garden and the 'great chapel' later built by Sixtus IV and commemorating his name. The

Sant'Angelo bridge would be the link between the sacred city and the profane, and the roads converging upon it from the east and those of the settlement across the Tiber would be straightened to lead up to the piazza in front of St Peter's, where Nero's obelisk would be placed. In this way the new artistic culture succeeded in ensuring continuity between the past and the future, identifying the new Rome with the ancient capital.

This programme was partially and slowly realized in the latter half of the fifteenth century. It was relaunched after the Jubilee of 1500 in a changed political and ideological atmosphere which gave new value to its intellectual ambition, while losing sight of the means realistically available. Julius II was able to employ the great artists coming from the schools of Florence and Urbino – Bramante, Michelangelo, Raphael – and their work initiated the 'third style' described by Vasari:[10] a universal synthesis of the visual and symbolic heritage accumulated in the *grand atelier d'Italie*,[11] which would stand from then on as a model for the civilized society of Europe.

The achievements of this period of intense activity were interrupted by the sack of 1527, which brought out above all the disproportion between imagination and reality: the gigantic St Peter's designed by Bramante remained unfinished for a century and a half; the straightened roads of Julius II (Via Giulia, Via della Lungara) and of Leo X (the trident starting from the Piazza del Popolo) stood as isolated exercises in perspective; the unfinished base of the Palazzo dei Tribunali stood out in the Via Giulia like an ancient ruin. The seeds of the impossible *renovatio* – Bramante's *tempietto* on the site of St Peter's crucifixion, the frescos of Michelangelo and Raphael – are guarded like undetonated bombs in the courtyard of San Pietro in Montorio, in the Sistine Chapel, and in the Vatican *Stanze*; their dialogue with the world continues beyond the limitations of time and space.

Only later and according to more modest aspirations would the modern systemization of Rome be completed, with the funereal imprint of Michelangelo and the festive, scrupulously historical one of Bernini. Rome would become, as we shall see, a capital like the others, but with the added testimony of a universal dream buried in the past.

Among Italian cities, only Venice, city of the eternal present, surpasses Rome in its uniqueness, which places it beyond comparison. The greatest Florentine artists gathered in Venice – Ghiberti in 1424, Paolo Uccello between 1425 and 1431, Michelozzo in 1433, Alberti in 1437, Andrea del Castagno in 1442 (also in Padua), Filippo Lippi in 1434, Donatello from 1443 on, Paolo Uccello again in 1445 – while the local ruling class resisted the spread of Tuscan influence and stuck proudly to its traditional models. Completion of the Piazzetta side of the Ducal Palace was begun in 1424 and continued throughout the remainder of the century in keeping with the Gothic style of that portion facing the quay. Even the reconstruction following the 1577 fire followed the original style.

This sort of resistance was first overcome in the field of painting. The collaboration of Antonio Vivarini, Giovanni d'Alemagna and Andrea Mantegna, begun in 1440, on the Eremitani Church in Padua initiated an intense artistic exchange which included Mantua, Ferrara and, by way of Piero della Francesca, the international environment of Urbino. Antonello da Messina, who had learned the new Flemish techniques of painting in Naples, arrived in 1475. His meeting with Giovanni Bellini was decisive for the birth of the Venetian school of painting; Carpaccio got his start there in 1488, Giorgione, Lotto and Titian in the last years of the century. Technical innovations – canvases, oils – and painting 'without a design' shifted the traditional balance of visual culture and gave first place to painting, no longer based on that 'design' common to the three arts.

Painting is the eye that sees, records and orders the visible world. The large canvases of Gentile Bellini and Carpaccio reproduce Venice in all its particulars and at the height of its prosperity. The 200 printing shops established after 1469 – including the fine one of Aldo Manuzio in 1490 – together with the engraving workshops continued to spread this imposing image. In 1500 Jacopo de' Barberi published his splendid and realistic panoramic view of the city.

Only at the end of the fifteenth century and in the first decades of the sixteenth did those masters drawn from Urbino – the Lombardos, Mauro Cordussi – and from Rome – Jacopo Sansovino – undertake the structural renewal of the city. The prestige and flexibility of the 'third style' made possible a confrontation with the continuity of tradition and the strict functional requirements of the canal city. The results of this grafting operation adorn the sides of the new Piazza San Marco: the old and new law courts,

48   Venice: Piazza San Marco, laid out in the sixteenth century (photo: Fotocielo, no. 381).

the library, and the loggia, which reproduce in a uniform and regular way the original porticoed deployment and surround the extraordinary three-dimensional organism of the church. The risks attendant upon a 'renewal' of this sort, considered by Tafuri,[12] were enormous. Palladio – curator of the San Marco basilica after 1570 – later found an outlet for his architecture in the great open spaces of the lagoon in which one sees reflected the churches of San Giorgio Maggiore, the Redentore and the Zitelle.

Alfonso I of Aragon, who conquered the kingdom of Naples in 1442, and Francesco Sforza, Duke of Milan from 1450, belong together with Leonello and Borso d'Este, Federico di Montefeltro and Gianfrancesco Gonzaga to the generation educated by the humanists. But Naples and Milan were large and unstable cities in which 'modern' modifications were necessarily isolated and the princes' palaces – the Castel Nuovo and the Castello Sforzesco – stood as disconnected quadrilaterals in intentional counterpoint to the city.

Sforza, allied with the Medici, brought Filarete to Milan from Florence for the building of the Ospedale Maggiore (1460–5); the Medici themselves sent Michelozzo to rebuild the palazzo of the Medici bank and the Portinari Chapel of Sant'Eustorgio. Later, Lorenzo il Magnifico sent Leonardo da Vinci in 1481 and Giuliano da Sangallo in 1493 to Ludovico il Moro. These contacts, while decisive for the shift of artistic culture they represented, did not lead to significant alterations in the shape of the Lombard capital, and the reflections of both Filarete and Leonardo regarding the city remained theoretical.

In Naples Alfonso II, who in 1465 married Ippolita, the daughter of Francesco Sforza, maintained close ties between his court and those of Florence and Milan, and employed some of the most celebrated artists from the north: Giuliano da Maiano in 1485 for the suburban villas of Poggioreale and of the Duchess and the Bolla aqueduct; Giuliano da Sangallo in 1488 for the new Palazzo dei Tribunali; Francesco di Giorgio in 1491 for the new western walls and the fortifications. Giovanni Pontano, who lived in Naples from 1448 to 1503, was the technical consultant for these works. Pontano himself together with Sannazzaro built two classically inspired villas in the region. In the poem *Lepidina* (1496), the Aragonese works were celebrated by means of a mythical account of the city's origin. Invasion by Charles VIII of

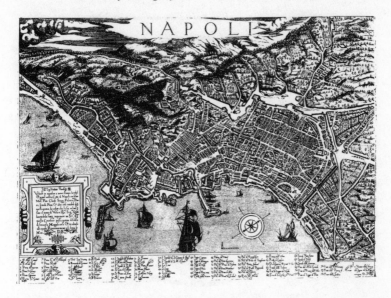

49   Naples: bird's-eye view by Donato Bertelli, c.1585.

France in 1495 ended this cycle of works, which may have aimed at the eventual total redesign of the city (referred to by Pietro Summonte in 1524). Within the context of the international empire of Charles V, Naples was enlarged and systemized by the Spanish viceroys of the sixteenth century, employing greater resources while ignoring the intellectual concerns of the previous century.

The Separation of Theory and Practice

The urban transformations carried out between the second half of the fourteenth century and the first half of the fifteenth, both in Italy and in the rest of Europe, were limited and intermittent, and certainly not in keeping with the ambitions of the new artistic culture, sure of the universal application of its design principles. While this culture did not ignore the problem of cities altogether, it did lack concrete experience with the use of technical, economic and administrative tools. It was in the figurative arts and in books that research on new urban models was pursued, research that sped out of control, ever more removed from the real world.

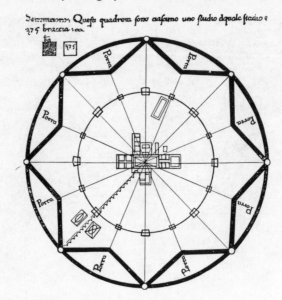

50 Sforzinda (illustration from Filarete's treatise, c.1460).

The careful balance between theory and practice still present in the mid-fifteenth-century treatise of Alberti was lost in the following decades. The treatise of Filarete,[13] written in Milan between 1460 and 1465, describes an imaginary city called Sforzinda; that of Francesco di Giorgio, written between 1470 and 1480 and dedicated to the Duke of Urbino, attempts a survey of the ideal city in various forms. The designs included with these treatises superseded the written texts. Perspective drawings of model cities appeared in the illustrated editions of Vitruvius, Fra Giocondo (1511), Cesariano (1521), Caporali (1536), Martin (1547), and Barbaro and Palladio (1556). It was, however, in painting that impossible environments and cityscapes took shape: in the backgrounds of the 'histories' and even in images specifically depicting groups of buildings in perspective, like the Baltimore and Berlin paintings of Urbino. Imagination lost touch with the real requirements of building, and theoretical research found application, after the mid-sixteenth century, only in the area of military architecture as new fortified cities became necessary along all the borders of Europe: Vitry-le-François and Villefranche-sur-Meuse

51   The Château de Chambord (photo: Benevolo).

(1545), Guastalla (1549), Charlemont and Philippeville (1555), La Valletta (1566), Zamosc (1578), Palmanova (1593), and Coerworden (1597).

While military engineers tackled the problems presented by this area of graphic design, writers expressed scepticism about the possible creation of new perfect models. Abandoning the realm of real physical settings, they employed 'utopias' in order to pass ironic or bitter judgement on the contradictions of the contemporary world: Doni (1548), Patrizi (1552), Agostini (1583),[14] Campanella (1602). The aged Campanella, having passed from prison to prison, arrived in Paris in 1638 and dedicated the definitive edition of his *City of the Sun* to the newborn son of Louis XIII, who would himself become the Sun King:

> Admirandam urbem, Solis de nomine dictam,
> me signasse tibi, puer, alto ex corde resigno.[15]

(This wondrous city, bearing the sun's name, I declare dedicated to you, O child, with all my heart.)

The search for new urban models degenerated in this way before practical applications could be sufficiently tested. This handicap of theory with respect to practice would subsequently endure and has still not been resolved, as we shall see below.

4

Confrontation with the World

Between 1434, when Gil Eannes rounded Cape Bojador, and the mid-sixteenth century, when the entire world was open to European colonization and trade, the 'disenclavement' of Europe took place as separate local worlds were combined into a single universe.[1]

French historians have attempted to measure in this regard the pressure exerted by a 'full' Europe on the rest of the world: 70–80

52 Antwerp: the town hall fire, 1576.

million people on 2.5 million sq km and concentrated around 130,000 towns. This 22–25 per cent of humanity consumed 50 per cent of the available animal protein and had access to five times the per capita energy available in China. It inhabited a continuous territory and from the top of any bell tower one could see four or five others. A critical mass had been reached so that this population sought outlets beyond its borders and came into contact with the rest of the world's population. The various human societies, separated from the dawn of history, were for the first time brought together and their differences became not only cause for conflict but also reason for success or failure.

There were cultural confrontations in addition to the material ones. Between 1405 and 1433 the Chinese Emperor Yung-lo sent a series of commercial and military maritime expeditions into the Indian Ocean, which, in spite of their overwhelmingly superior means and equipment, were called off for lack of interest in external contacts. The Chinese world sought to preserve its internal equilibrium while the European world found its own equilibrium by embracing the entire planet and establishing a 'world economy'.[2]

The tight European constellation of large and small cities was one of the factors in this confrontation. The contrast between European settlement models and those encountered elsewhere is especially important and fertile in consequences. In those areas where this encounter was fully played out – in the Americas – it led to enormous destruction and suffering, but also significant verification, rethinking and adaptation. Our task is to place these events in an objective historical setting, and to evaluate the differences that went into these clashes as elements of a precious human heritage, elements left in disarray but not entirely lost.

For this purpose all terms of the conflict must be re-evaluated, both the intellectual and material means of the colonizers and the situation in each region subject to European penetration.

The European Resources Employed Overseas

In addition to measuring as a whole the differences between Europe and the other worlds, we need to consider the meagre material and intellectual resources employed in this encounter.

It was Portugal, a small peripheral country, that for a century led the way in oceanic exploration. Neither sufficiently rich nor sufficiently populous to conquer vast territories, Portugal sought to establish a network of commercial bases on the route to the Indies and so to control the supply of spices reaching Antwerp and the European market. Spain, larger and wealthier, entered the competition later, seeking with Columbus to arrive at the same goal by travelling west. The 1494 Treaty of Tordesillas, sponsored by Pope Alexander VI, fixed the longitude of demarcation between the two powers. The presence of an immense colonizable continent in the western hemisphere, reserved for Spain, was only discovered later; and the Catholic Monarchs dedicated scant attention and means to this undertaking. Political, economic and cultural attention was always centred on internal affairs. Only the occasional echo from this great overseas adventure arrived to disturb the European debate, a debate to which the actors in this adventure made only limited contributions: the geometric spirit implicit in navigational techniques, war, and business, and the curiosity and daring of rushing headlong into the unknown.

For our purposes, the logic behind the settlements was that same schematic and utilitarian attitude which dominated the centres of economic and military power in the first half of the sixteenth century: on one side the Bairro Alto of Lisbon (1513), the Fuggerei of Augsburg (1514) and the expansion of Antwerp after 1540; on the other the last internal colonial cities – Cortemaggiore (1479), Valbonne (1519) – and the encampment cities – Puerto Real (1483) and Santa Fè de Granada (1492) – built by the Catholic Monarchs during the war against the Moors. These were all products of a general *esprit de géometrie* in which the persistent medieval tradition harmonized with the humanist preference for regularity. The technicians who embarked upon these ocean voyages took with them a similar mentality, but also a certain provincialism as if to provide a degree of psychological protection in the face of the distances travelled and the risks encountered. The Portuguese founded new cities on sites where the familiar medieval model of their homeland could be reproduced, a landing place combined with higher ground – Angra in the Azores, Cape Town, Sao Paolo de Luanda, Bahia, Macao – while the Spanish carefully reproduced in Mexico and Peru the urban settings of Andalusia and Estremadura, including even the late Gothic – Huejtozingo, Calpan – and

Muslim styles – Cholula – or models taken from the illustrations of Renaissance treatises – Actopan, Quito.

Looked at from another point of view, the overseas expeditions required an enormous expenditure of physical and mental energy. The clash over control of the passages to the Indies, after the voyage of Vasco da Gama in 1498, occurred in a brief stretch of time and over a vast area: in 1500, Alvarez Cabral landed on the coast of Brazil initiating another gigantic and unintentional process of colonization. And in 1502, Vasco da Gama led an armed fleet and attacked the Arab ships carrying spices in the Red Sea and Persian Gulf, from where they travelled by land to Venetian-controlled ports on the Mediterranean. Alfonso de Albuquerque arrived in India in 1503, seized the Arab ports of Socotra (1506) and Ormuz (1507) and in 1509 destroyed the Arab fleet in battle. In this same period the Venetians were studying a plan to cut through the Suez Isthmus, abandoned because of war with the League of Cambrai. Albuquerque then founded the base of Goa in 1510, conquered Malacca in 1511 and opened the way to Indonesia and China. He arrived in Canton in 1513, and established the first contacts with the Ming Empire. Prior to his death in 1515, he proposed a plan for the definitive elimination of Arab competition: he would import workers familiar with excavation from the sugar works in the Azores to divert the Nile into the Red Sea, and also to steal the body of Mohammed from Mecca so that it could be offered in exchange for the liberation of Jerusalem. In Camoes's poem *Os Lusíadas*, written in the mid-sixteenth century, these events are fabulously described, like the adventures of medieval knights recounted by Ariosto or Boiardo.[3]

With a few hundred armed men, Hernando Cortés conquered the Aztec Empire in 1519–22, the years during which Magellan completed his trip around the world. Francisco Pizarro accomplished a similar feat against the Incan Empire in 1532–7. The *conquistadores* encountered what Teràn has called the 'tropicalization of the white man'.[4] Alvaro Nuñes Cabeza de Vaca led the first exploration of the plains of North America in 1528 and left a description of that voyage: he and two companions, after having lost their clothes, lived naked for six years among the Indians, 'and being unaccustomed to this practice, our skin shed twice a year.' When they returned to Mexico in 1534, they were unable to get used to wearing clothes again. Along with the adventurers, traders and fortune-seekers who came from all parts of Europe in this period, the first missionaries sent to Cortés by Charles V in 1523 were three Flemings chosen by Adrian VI, including Peter of Ghent, and in 1524 the 'twelve' led by Fray Martín de Valencia who had studied at the universities of Salamanca, Alcalà and the Sorbonne. In 1526 the Dominicans of Fray Domingo de Batanzos arrived, 'the radical churchmanship of Cisneros'.[5] In 1515 Las Casas opened the controversy over colonization methods which he followed up in Salamanca in 1539 and brought to the *nuevas leyes* in 1542. The unfortunate clash between two distant cultures – 'so diametrically opposed to each other through their different conditions that the first people to become aware of the fact could not believe that they were both equally human' – took place for better or worse in extreme conditions:

> A continent barely touched by man lay exposed to men whose greed could no longer be satisfied by their own continent. Everything would be called into question . . . everything would be verified in practice and revoked in principle: the Garden of Eden, the Golden Age of Antiquity, the Fountain of Youth, Atlantis, the Hesperides, the Islands of the Blessed, would be found to be true, but revelation, salvation, customs and law would be challenged by the spectacle of a purer, happier race of men (who, of course, were not really purer or happier, although a deep-seated remorse made them appear so). Never had humanity experienced such a harrowing test.[6]

The Colonization of Asia and Africa

The existing trade routes followed by the Europeans skirted both sub-Saharan Africa and southern Asia. The first was a continent impenetrable to the white race: in 1485 Diego Cao led an expedition up the Congo River, and Francisco Barreto ventured up the Zambezi in 1569, but both voyages fell victim to malaria. Further exploration would have to await the discovery of quinine in the first half of the nineteenth century. In southern Asia the Europeans encountered well-populated and fairly advanced states. The failed occupation of Calicut demonstrated the impossibility of conquest, and the Europeans coexisted with the Asian kingdoms, taking a few coastal landings for themselves.

The *Estado de India* was the heart of the Portuguese Empire, which is to say the chain of territories along the western coast of the Indian peninsula. Goa, the capital, was occupied in 1510, already one of the most important Indian ports and trading centres. The city, together with a small surrounding territory, functioned as an indigenous state on the edge of the Hindu Empire of Vijayanagar. From Goa the Portuguese viceroy could deal with the Asian sovereigns according to traditional practices. The voyage from Goa to Lisbon was regulated by the monsoons and lasted one year. Each year a fleet of five or six ships left Lisbon with 10,000 tons of merchandise and 3,000 men; of the latter less than 2,000 arrived safe and sound in Goa.

The *Estado*, in which the Portuguese able to bear arms numbered no more than six or seven thousand, was founded upon a compromise that determined the architecture of the city as well. The Portuguese protected local customs, recognized in the *foral* of 1526, and at the same time carefully sought to reproduce European municipal institutions. From the beginning Goa shared the laws of Lisbon. The first hospice for the poor was created in 1520, and the first bishopric in 1538. The viceroy maintained a sumptuous court to impress his visitors, and the Portuguese merchants consumed there the better part of their profits. The luxurious and reckless life of Goa, 'Babylon of the East' according to Camoes, became proverbial.

The compact plan of the Indian settlement, adopted with minor variations, was strangely similar to that of Lisbon with its steep narrow streets, a fact noted by English voyagers of the seventeenth century with disapproval. Christian sanctuaries were erected next to Hindu temples: the cathedral was founded in 1511 and the Franciscan monastery begun in 1517. The leading Portuguese painter of the day, Garcia Fernandes, worked on the cathedral between 1538 and 1540. From 1521 cargoes of Chinese porcelain arrived, which influenced Portuguese painting of the period. In 1542 Francisco Saverio came and described the marvellous heterogeneity of this unique city, the only example of a serious attempt to allow the coexistence of European and Asian traditions.

In that same year the new viceroy, de Souza, proposed reorganization of the *Estado*, and the Jesuits introduced a vast programme for spreading the Christian faith throughout the Asian continent. The bishop of Goa became the eastern primate, pagan temples were closed, and the Inquisition was introduced. In spite of competition for trade with Europe, Goa remained the major centre for Asian traffic. In this period the city's most important monuments were built – Santa Catarina in 1551, Bom Jesus in 1594 – and *Goa dourado* reached its maximum splendour, while losing much of its integrated character.

The Spanish occupied the Philippines in 1565 and carried out a systematic colonization similar to that practised in America. The capital, Manila, was laid out in 1571 according to urban regulations codified contemporaneously in the *Leyes de India* (1573). The Portuguese founded the commercial base of Macao in 1557 on a promontory near Canton, and between 1587 and 1594 occupied Ceylon, where they founded the port city of Colombo. The Dutch arrived in the Indian Ocean in 1595, and in 1614 they founded Batavia in Java. In 1641 they took Malacca from the Portuguese and, as a concession from the Shogun, acquired the island of Deshima near Nagasaki in order to conduct limited trading with Japan, otherwise closed to foreigners. The English entered the picture as well in this period, founding Madras (1647), Bombay (1665) and Calcutta (1691) on the Indian coast. The French founded Pondicherry in 1677.

Many of these cities, which would subsequently grow out of all measure, were fortresses built according to the rules of European military architecture. Little heed was taken of the existing urban settlements, and the European cities existed separately from the previously existing indigenous ones. This isolation allowed for unlimited transplantings from the colonizers' homelands. Batavia, the capital of the Dutch East Indies, was modelled after Delft, with a network of navigable canals and quays. The canals, however, became infested with crocodiles, and the stagnant water made the city uninhabitable. It was reconstructed elsewhere in the nineteenth century. Governor Lenoir sumptuously expanded Pondicherry between 1721 and 1735 according to models from the French courts: straight boulevards and *ronds points* provided access to the manufactures and villages in the surrounding swamps. Full confrontation with Asian civilizations and their settlements, however, would not take place until the nineteenth century.

The Colonization of the New World

Upon learning of the existence of great empires in the new continent, the Spanish, already settled in the Antilles, made contact with an advanced culture, but one which paradoxically was defenceless against European aggression. Comparison of the great monumental American settlements, which amazed the chroniclers of the European conquests, with the Eurasian cities lacked even a common lexicon. The transition which subjugated the city to its surrounding territory had not taken place in the New World. The central loci of the two empires – Tenochtitlan and Cuzco – were monumental projections, perceived as directly relating to the immense surrounding spaces which coincided subjectively with the world. These were the last products of the Neolithic ability to occupy and model an unlimited space, coincidentally part of a world that had been urbanized for 4,000 years. The Spanish, who compared these cities to those in Spain, were struck by their gigantic scale, and by their visual freedom and magnificence, but their appeal was a forgotten one, coming from a remote age. They were able neither to use nor to comprehend these cities, and succeeded only in destroying them.

The Aztec capital, Tenochtitlan, was a ceremonial centre set in the middle of a lagoon. Its extent was approximately 750 hectares and included two distinct parts: the public spaces, temples and palaces on the naturally formed islands (about 190 hectares) and the dwellings built on artificial islands (*chinampas*, about 560 hectares). The three dike-bridges that connected these to the mainland converged toward the pyramid-shaped temples of the central nucleus, visual focus of the entire setting. The population struck the first chroniclers as enormous and has been estimated at about 60,000. Numerous boats provided transportation. Accounts include descriptions of combined water and land communication that recall Venice: 'There are three types of roads: the first of water spanned by many bridges, the second of land, occasionally interrupted as water runs between them, and the third . . . of water and land both to accommodate equally pedestrians and boats'; and 'houses normally have two doors, one opening on to the street, the other on to the water.' Also referred to are the infrequent cleaning of houses and streets (on the occasion of the resupplying of water

53 *Mexico: the Aztec lake city (engraving by G. Ramusio, 1565).*

from Chapultapec, that passed along two parallel conduits on the western dike-bridge – 'when one became dirty, the other was used') and the lively market square.

This delicate ecosystem fell into ruin immediately after the conquest. The lagoon receded from 1524.[7] In 1568 Diaz de Castillo wrote, 'This city is lost, razed to the ground.'[8] In fact, Cortés's *xumetrico* (surveyor), Alonso Garcia Bravo, laid out the viceroy's capital along the lines of the Aztec capital, while employing a European conceptual repertory: streets, squares, building lots. Subsequent descriptions praised the regularity of the *traza* with its 'lovely wide and long streets, apparently made following a single model'.[9] Part of the central area became an immense square of over 7 hectares, the *zocalo*. The lagoon was pushed back away from the inhabited area, and in the seventeenth century was entirely reclaimed by Flemish experts. On its site would develop the huge present-day city which covers every vestige of the original setting.

The Incan empire consisted of the known world from the equator south including 6,000 km of coast and stretching from the Pacific to the Amazon forest. It was criss-crossed by a network of

54   Cholula (photo: Cia Mexicana Aerofoto).

footpaths that converged upon Cuzco (which means 'navel'). The capital was situated on a small plateau between two rivers at an elevation of 3,300 m. At the foot of rocky slopes, this mountain setting was only slightly modified by the terraces of freestone that marked the limits of the temples and palaces, the latter topped with thatched roofs. The Sacsahuaman fortress, located over the town, was defended from above by an extraordinary triple saw-tooth fortification. The main square, Huacapata, was a 500 by 250-m rectangle linking the city and the open countryside. It was traversed by the channelled course of the River Huatanay. The stone work was so boldly standardized that a European observer remarked that 'a single architect seems to have planned all of the many monuments.'[10]

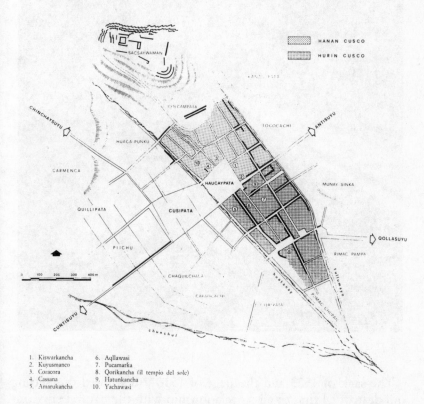

1. Kiswarkancha
2. Kuyusmanco
3. Coracora
4. Cassana
5. Amarukancha
6. Aqllawasi
7. Pucamarka
8. Qorikancha (il tempio del sole)
9. Hatunkancha
10. Yachawasi

55 *Map of Cuzco, showing the surviving Inca structures (from G. Gasparini,* Arquitectura Inka, *Caracas, 1977).*

The sack of 1533 and the siege of 1536–7 disrupted this setting and destroyed first of all its relationship with the natural environment. In 1548 Cieza de León wrote: 'Today the river is full of dung and garbage; in the time of the Incas it was limpid and clean; the water ran over slabs of stone . . . and many times Spaniards found

56 (opposite and above) Two streets in Cuzco, following the course of streets of the Inca capital (photos: Benevolo).

small gold ornaments that bathers had lost.'[11] The Spanish city was built on top of that of the Incas; the enormous Plaza de Armas covered only part of the Huacatapa, while the Incan walls served as foundations for the whitewashed walls of the houses and convents. The ancient stone setting, however, built into the mountain, endured, and the splendid and precisely carved curtains have emerged unscathed through periodic earthquakes.

The destruction and reconstruction of these two capitals presaged the general transformation of settlements in the Americas. In 1555 the first council of the Mexican Church resolved that the indigenous peoples 'be persuaded – or forced if necessary, but with the minimum possible violence – to congregate in convenient locations and in cities where they can live in a civil and Christian way.'[12] This operation, referred to as *poblar*, formed much of the basis for relations between Europeans and the local populations. It became necessary to found many new cities and – according to the instructions received by Pedraris Davila in 1513 – 'Towns being newly founded may be established according to plan without difficulty. If not started with form they will never attain it.'[13]

In 1525 Cortés issued instructions that make reference to a standardized model:

> Having felled the trees, you must begin to clear the territory and then, following the plan I have devised, trace out the public spaces: the plaza, the church, the town hall, the prison, the market, the butcher's, the hospital ... Then you must indicate to each citizen his assigned lot, according to the plan, and you will do likewise for those who come subsequently. Be certain that the roads are straight and find surveyors capable of laying these out.[14]

His surveyor, Garcia Bravo, drew up not only the plan for Mexico City, but also those for Vera Cruz and Oaxaca. Other planners included Alonso Martin Perez (Puebla, 1531), Juan Alanis (Queretaro, 1534) and Juan Ponce (Morelia, 1541). In 1531 Pizarro founded the first Spanish city in Peru – San Miguel, 'according to the rule, with a central plaza' – and later, following the same model, Quito (1532) and Lima (1535).

In the southern viceroyalty, systematic concentration of population in the new cities dates from 1570, after the arrival of the new

57   *Plan for Santiago de Leon (Caracas), 1567 (Archivio de Indias, Seville).*

viceroy, Toledo, and the execution of the last of the Incas, Tupac Amaru. The latter act was intended to destroy indigenous unity and quell potential revolts. Settlement was generally shifted from hilly areas to the lower plains, to which the natives adapted poorly. The ancient network of settlements linked by footpaths, cities clinging to the mountains (Pisac), and the cultivated terraces (*andenerias*) lining their slopes were abandoned. Like Cuzco, however, they endured and have re-emerged intact following recent exploration.

The widespread (and onerous) practice of founding new cities led to occasional innovation. During the first phase of Mexican colonization, a huge open structure formed the heart of the new communities. This consisted of an *atrio*, an enclosed courtyard; the *posas*, small chapels for the processions; and the *capella de indios*, a sort of daytime apse for saying mass to large groups. In 1531, at the age of seventy, Judge Vasco de Quiroga arrived in Mexico. He sold off his possessions to build two ideal cities based on Thomas More's *Utopia* in which the Indians lived and worked. In 1541 he became bishop of Patzcuaro and built a cathedral able to accommodate all 30,000 inhabitants in five radial sections converging toward a central altar.

In 1571, after hundreds of cities had already been founded, the general procedure was given detailed codification in a law for the purpose:

> On arriving at the locality where the new settlement is to be founded (which according to our will and ordinance must be one which is vacant and can be occupied without doing harm to the Indians and natives or with their free consent) the plan of the place, with its squares, streets and building lots is to be outlined by means of measuring with a cord and ruler, beginning with the main square from which streets are to run to the gates and principal roads and leaving sufficient open space so that even if the town grows it can always spread in a symmetrical manner . . . The main plaza should be in the centre of the town and of an oblong shape, its length being equal to at least one and a half times its width, as this proportion is the best for festivals in which horses are used and any other celebrations which have to be held . . . The plaza is to be planned with reference to the possible growth of the town. It shall not be smaller than two hundred feet wide

and three hundred feet long nor larger than eight hundred feet long and three hundred feet wide. A well-proportionated medium-size plaza is one six hundred feet long and four hundred feet wide.

From the plaza the four principal streets are to diverge, one from the middle of each of its sides and two streets are to meet at each of its corners. The four corners of the plaza are to face the four points of the compass, because thus the streets diverging from the plaza will not be directly exposed to the four principal winds, which would cause much inconvenience ... The eight streets which run into the plaza at its four corners are to do so freely without being obstructed by the arcades of the plaza ... In cold climates the streets shall be wide; in hot climates narrow; however, for purposes of defense and where horses are kept the streets had better be wide ... In inland towns the church is not to be on the plaza but at a distance from it in a situation where it can stand by itself, separate from other buildings so that it can be seen from all sides ... It would be built on high ground so that in order to reach its entrance people will have to ascend a flight of steps ... The hospital of the poor who are ill with non-contagious diseases shall be built facing the north, and so planned that it will enjoy a southern exposure ... No building lots surrounding the main plaza are to be given to private individuals for these are to be reserved for the church, Royal and Town house, also shops and dwellings for the merchants ... The remaining building lots shall be distributed by lottery to those of the settlers who are entitled to build around the main plaza. Those left over are to be held for us to grant to settlers who may come later or dispose of at our pleasure ... The building lots and the structures erected thereon are to be so situated that in the living rooms one can enjoy air from the south and from the north ... Settlers are to endeavor, as far as possible, to make all structures uniform, for the sake of the beauty of the town.[15]

Although some of the regulations regarding orientation and winds are theoretical in character, and for that reason not generally applicable to every kind of site, this law formalized an elementary and widespread model. Historians have discussed a number of equally possible sources: the interrupted but not forgotten tradition of the medieval new cities, the ancient models described in treatises on architecture and the military arts, and symmetrical designs taken from modern treatises. The geometric mentality of the Renaissance had already become widespread and ingrained, necessary for the functioning of industry, trade, exploration and business; in the daily environments of work and relaxation, it was psychologically reassuring.

The rules of planning imported by the Europeans served as both functional tools and a sign of identification, a profound link to the cultural traditions of the homeland. There was, however, in all this a disastrous distribution of energy and talent. While the great European artists found no opportunity to experiment on an urban scale and instead pursued points of perfection which took them ever further from the central urban problems, the mediocre practitioners who embarked on the American voyages found themselves planning and building all at once entire cities for tens of thousands of inhabitants. From our point of view and perhaps in general, the result was an irreconcilably negative balance with regard to what was destroyed and what was built, a clear repudiation of the theoretical universality of the European models.

According to the wishes of their founders, the American colonial cities were in fact European cities transported over enormous distances. The repudiation referred to above is reflected in a combination of choices and omissions which can be summarized as follows:

1 The 'plan' defined at the moment of founding was a two-dimensional design, a *traza* on which, as in the Middle Ages, building would not take place all at once. Building lots were assigned, and those holding title would begin construction when they saw fit and in whatever way they wanted. The design of the streets and the plazas was often unnecessarily large, while the buildings were low and undistinguished, usually only a single storey high. Alternatively, a modest design, for example that of Buenos Aires in 1583, might underestimate the eventual importance of the city.

2 The eventual size of the city was unknown. As a result, the grid could be extended in all directions as it gradually became necessary to add new blocks. The external limits of the cities were always temporary, in part because city walls were unnecessary; only in the late sixteenth century were a few coastal cities fortified.

The separation between city and country, so evident in Europe and especially in Spain, was lessened. Large open spaces within the cities, sometimes a vast network of streets, frequently lay idle and without structures (Cholula).

3   The uniformity of the grid, often decided at the desk of a bureaucrat, prevented natural adaptation to the terrain and gave a monotonous quality to the urban setting. Ironically, these cities acquired a degree of character when incorporating a previous design (as at Cuzco), or else thanks to a failure to stake out a rugged terrain properly. Suitable formal elaboration would follow when these settings had been lived in and humanized. It was out of this latter process that sprang the originality in architecture and the figurative arts of the seventeenth and eighteenth centuries, often the work of indigenous artists in whom an inherited cultural tradition manifested itself in unexpected ways.

The model given currency by the Spanish was applied without notable innovation by French, Dutch and English colonizers in the urbanization of North America. As in Portuguese Brazil, there was not even the question of confrontation with the tiny indigenous settlements dispersed here and there and leaving scarcely a trace. Various names – Mississippi, Chicago, Manhattan – recall an earlier human presence in these regions, but it is only recently that scholars have sought and documented the extraordinary earthen settings built in the Great Plains of the United States.

A Cartesian grid became the standard sign of civilization in even the most unexpected and inappropriate environments. These settings were of course determined by the initial choice of a favourable site for the founding of a city, generally a grand and complex geographical setting. The estuaries of great rivers along the Atlantic coast and the coast of the Gulf of Mexico (as on the Brazilian bays) were the dominating elements of these new urban scenarios: Montreal, Quebec, Boston, New York, Philadelphia, New Orleans, Maracaibo, Rio de Janeiro, Bahia.

Only at the end of the eighteenth century, in a new political and cultural climate, would the grid be reconceived on a geographical scale and become the universal tool for the division of any surface: a city, an agricultural region, a state, a continent. The Land Act championed by Jefferson in 1785 established a grid oriented along lines of latitude and longitude for the purpose of western colonization: each block contained 16 square miles and could be divided

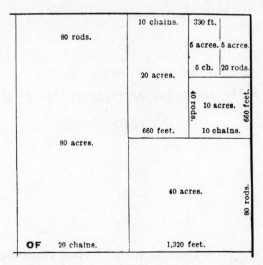

58   The land grid laid down by Thomas Jefferson's Ordinance (1785) and applied to the settlement of new territories in the United States.

into two, four, eight, sixteen, thirty-two or sixty-four smaller parts. This law received widespread application in the United States, and similar devices have been used in all parts of the world where it has been necessary to designate borders and divide up virgin territory.

As a result of this general approach, the link with European traditions was broken as early as the eighteenth century. The perspective grid, product of a particular visual education, became an abstract technique linked to scientific culture and allowed human calculation to seize control of all terrestrial space. The effects of this development are printed on the maps of the United States and of any part of the world, save Europe.

Having developed these tools, Europe none the less remains the only part of the world in which the effects of the laws of perspective are not visible on a geographical scale, or from a satellite, but only on a topographical scale, that is from a vantage point that does not lose contact with the view from ground level. The adaptation of the European setting to the rules of perspective opened a long and eventful debate that we shall attempt to recount in the following chapter.

5

The Difficult Adjustment to the Laws
of Perspective

The New Conditions for Urban Planning

After the Treaty of Cateau-Cambrésis (1559) and the Council of
Trent (1563) had established a relatively stable political and
religious balance in Europe, a new phase of reorganization began, a
phase reflected in urban and territorial settlement.

The courts became firmly established in the cities, which in turn
became national capitals. Military resources were employed in
fortifying cities and borders, while civil and military shipping
needs required the planning and modernization of ports. Technological progress, population growth, increased financial activity,
bureaucratization, specialization and the need to represent new
public and private interests by means of external forms all contributed to an extensive process of urban renewal.

Beginning in 1530 Rome underwent a functional restructuring
commensurate with its role as the Papal See, and Florence was
fitted out as the capital of the Medici dukedom. The French court
came to Paris in 1528, when Francis I began the reconstruction of
the Louvre castle. Philip II chose Madrid as his capital in 1561, but
began construction on the Escorial palace-monastery in the mountains north of Madrid in 1562. The House of Savoy established
itself in Turin in 1563, which was then enlarged in 1620, 1673 and
1714. In the second half of the sixteenth century the Spanish
viceroys rebuilt the cities of Palermo and Naples, trading centres
and military bases of their Mediterranean empire. In London, the

Stuart court took up residence in Westminster, and the City was rebuilt after the fire of 1666. The Habsburgs came to Vienna only in 1683, after the defeat of the Turks at Kahlenberg.

The principal mercantile cities of the early sixteenth century – Genoa, Messina, Lisbon, Antwerp, Lyon, Augsburg – also acquired a new and more important architectural organization in this period; and the Low Countries, which emerged as a force in the world economy in the first half of the seventeenth century, enlarged their splendid port cities. In the late sixteenth and early seventeenth centuries, the kings of Sweden and Denmark expanded their capitals and founded many new cities. The Russian Tsar Ivan IV (1533–84) rebuilt Moscow and began colonization of the Urals.

Our intention here is to identify, both in Europe and America, the applications and experimental confirmations of perspective as a characteristic element of European culture. Material and social conditions had changed. In the new political and economic setting, financial means had increased, construction technology had developed, and artistic culture had passed beyond the threshold of the third style. The search for future perfection gave way to the backward-looking and more reassuring vision of an inherited system of rules and models. It was above all the birth of modern science that altered the task of Renaissance visual culture. Art no longer claimed objective correspondence with the real world, as this reality was now analysable by other methods which employed a different category of evidence. As Jaspers has put it with regard to Leonardo, 'to know' no longer meant 'to represent', but to discover the mechanical laws which governed the world of appearances. Mathematics, rather than geometry, was the tool of this project, and the crucial experiment, rather than subjective evaluation, confirmed its results. As artistic culture lost the certainty of its objectivity, it moved into the world of sentiment and morality, taking on the collection of values that science was eliminating from its domain.

This basic change profoundly altered the balance of architectural choice. So long as the rules of antiquity and those of perspective, combined from the time of Brunelleschi, were considered to have an objective basis, their application legitimated in a way the nature of things and confirmed an already existing order. Architecture fitted into an established universal hierarchy: the unmoved mover, the concentric spheres, the sub-lunar world, the terrestrial world, and within this the world of human manufacture. The city found its place at the boundary of the last two spheres. The difficulty inherent in confronting the size of the city was implicitly justified by this hierarchy: the primary task of the architect was to scale external space to human measure and to arrange perceivable three-dimensional environments within the dimensional limits inherited from the ancient and medieval traditions.

But then Copernicus's treatise (1543) cast doubt upon the traditional astronomical hierarchy and Galileo's *Sidereus Nuncius* (1619) burst it apart. In the new universe, space was a single infinite medium, not a characteristic of the bodies occupying it and differentiated according to their qualities. Architecture had to find its place in this unlimited universe and was forced to employ its tools, the perspective arrangement of recognizable elements, in order to capture the new notion of the infinite. In this context, outside the boundaries of Classical space, the planning of cities and territory was attempted anew and the inconsistency between the existing medieval cities and the new requirements of visual culture became apparent.

It is the conflict arising out of the encounter of this attempt with the operational difficulties of European society in the two centuries between 1550 and 1750 that concerns us. In an age characterized by dissimulation, comments reflecting the true scale of this problem are remarkably infrequent, and often only hinted at, as in an enigmatic note found among Colbert's papers after his death in 1683: 'Plants partout à continuer. Arc de Triomphe pour les conquêtes de terre. Observatoire pour les cieux. Pyramide; difficultés à l'exécution.'[1]

The City in Perspective: Urban Transformation between 1550 and 1650

The 'modern' innovations conceived up to the mid-sixteenth century – Via Alessandrina, Via Giulia, Via della Lungara, the tridents converging on the Ponte Sant'Angelo and Piazza del Popolo in Rome; the roads of the grid expansions of Lisbon and Antwerp; the Via Nuova of Perugia and that of Genoa designed by Alessi; Via Toledo in Naples – served to line up a series of architectural elements on a single front. The assembling of short transverse perspectives took precedence over the establishment of a more elongated one. The most important architectural structures of the period – the princely galleries of the palaces along the Genoese Via Nuova – were found along the sides of these roads rather than at their ends, and the total length rarely exceeded 1 km. The two great perpendicular roads of the Erculea addition of Ferrara, measuring 2 and 1.3 km, are exceptions, but represent over-scaled planning and were only partially lined with buildings.

In the second half of the sixteenth century, the urban setting became a collective concern. Italian, German and Flemish engravers – Guicciardini in 1567, Lafréry around 1570, Van Deventeer from 1558 to 1572, Duchet around 1580, Bertelli around 1585, Van Aelst around 1590, Florimi in the first decade of the seventeenth century, Merian in 1615, Münster in 1628 – supplied the market with a large number of perspective city views in which a great deal of information was combined in a realistic rendering. For the first time the entire heritage of the European cities was precisely represented according to the tenets of Renaissance visual culture and given general circulation. The population became accustomed to the synthetic perception of the parts of the urban organism and the relationship between city and geographical setting.

Perspective, the tool used to create these images, was subsequently and consciously employed for the rectification of urban settings. The new rectilinear avenues became more frequent and longer, and better emphasized the view of the vanishing point. In the 1560s Pius IV renewed in Rome the ancient line leading from the Quirinal towards the Porta Nomentana and extended it 1600 metres to Michelangelo's Porta Pia. Between 1572 and 1590 Gregory XIII and Sixtus V created a new network of streets linking the basilicas on the eastern hills which included a straight and undulating road running for almost three kilometres from Trinità dei Monti to Santa Maria Maggiore and Santa Croce. The combination of these new roads with the straight roads of antiquity and the pontifical roads of the previous century traced a perspective triangulation on top of the medieval pattern, in which considerations of perspective had been entirely lacking, and allowed the visual connection of far-off points within the city. Reference points were identified with columns or ancient unearthed obelisks. Today these objects stand in formless open

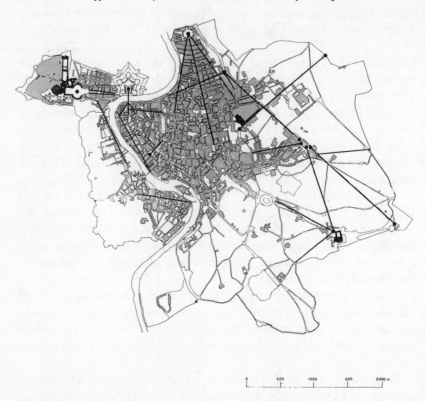

59   Rome: the straight thoroughfares opened up in the fifteenth and sixteenth centuries.

spaces, and the urban fabric is revealed only by a few constricted views narrowed down from their intended width.

The most ambitious project of this period was that of Palermo. Between 1564 and 1570 the port was expanded to the north-west, allowing the waterfront to serve as the monumental façade of this city on the sea, while the ancient longitudinal Cassero axis was extended to the shore. This straight avenue, 1.8 km long and rising by a total of 28 m, was the only opening in this city compacted by the subdivision of the last remaining free spaces within the city walls, the Papireto and the Magione. It was formalized in 1582–3 with the construction of two monumental gates: that towards the sea consisted of two wings separated to allow a view of the blue sea; that towards the mountain was topped by a pyramid which

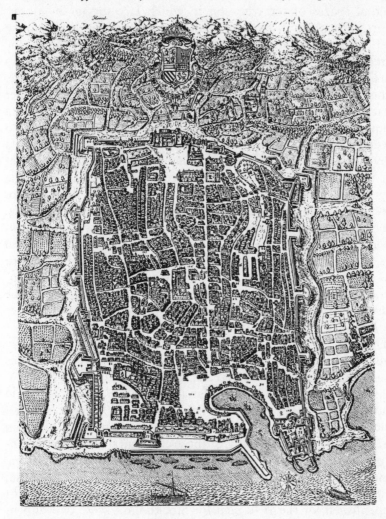

60   *Palermo: map by C. Duchet (1580), showing the straight avenue of the Cassero.*

served as a visual link with the road's continuation towards Monreale, where it ended at the foot of the hill after another 4.3 km.

This extraordinary perspective axis, over 6 km in length, was unified by a masterful visual treatment and inserted perfectly into the urban and territorial organism. It connects the principal

internal spaces of the city – on to which face the urban monuments, the cathedral, the Royal Palace, the Piazza Pretoria, and the
'Steri' (Palazzo Chiaramonte) – and leads resolutely from the
Tyrrhenian Sea to the island's mountainous interior. It has no
equal in Europe, and may have been born of the desire to achieve,
using modern methods, a level of greatness equal to that of earlier
great cities. The addition of a perpendicular road in 1597 – the Via
Maqueda – compromised somewhat this invention. The two
streets of equal width, their intersection richly decorated, create a
conventional cross, imposed with some difficulty on the asymmetric urban fabric. The almost level course of the Via Maqueda
intersected poorly with the two valleys parallel to the Cassero,
never becoming intelligible from a perspective point of view.
Paradoxically, it became important only in the nineteenth century,
when it was extended in both directions and became the principal
axis of the city. Subsequently the original design of the Cassero
was permanently corrupted by senseless contemporary development: the straight line to Monreale has been besieged by the
apartment houses of the periphery, and the new outer breakwater
has cut off the visual line to the sea.

During the building boom of the late sixteenth and early
seventeenth centuries, European sovereigns sponsored numerous
projects that brought symmetry and regularity to the large cities:
the royal *places* of Henri IV in Paris (1604–6), the Plaza Mayor in
Madrid (1617), the rebuilding of Lerma (1604), the prince's
residence at Charleville (1610), and the first expansion of Turin
(1620), where the uniformity of the architectural choices compensated for the uncertainty of the large-scale perspective composition.
Some projects – those that sought to encompass an urban organism
in its entirety like the 1620 plan for Göteborg, the 1629 plan for
Copenhagen, or the 1640 plan for Stockholm – were two-dimensional plans and translated into a structural setting only slowly and
incompletely. Absolutism demanded perfect and unquestioned
settings, a requirement compatible neither with the security of
formal choices nor with the mastery of technical, economic and
organizational tools.

In contrast with the capitals of the absolutist and mercantilist
regimes, the free Dutch cities managed a happy combination of
medieval administrative procedures and modern visual tools. The
seven provincial states, dominated by the mercantile bourgeoisie of

the major cities, competed victoriously with the great monarchies of the day and contributed to the birth of a global financial market that wreaked havoc with the national economies controlled from above. Their success depended upon a series of traditional institutions – communal, Burgundian, corporative – and anticipated the political and economic direction of eighteenth-century liberalism, skipping over, as Huizinga suggests, the mercantilist phase. Under cover of these 'freedoms', the most advanced experiments of European literature, art and science found shelter. In De Witt's time, Rembrandt, Huygens and Spinoza all worked contemporaneously in Amsterdam, while the writings of Descartes and Galileo were being published there.

Originality of this sort was fully confirmed in the systemization of rural and urban areas. The land itself was the product of human intervention which intensified in the second half of the sixteenth century after the disastrous floods of the first half (1508 and 1532). Between 1540 and 1640 approximately 120,000 hectares were reclaimed by the drying up of internal basins, and another 45,000 in the following century. City development depended upon reclamation of the surrounding land and was necessarily the product of the collective planning of concerted actions.

The revolt against Spanish domination lasted from 1565 to 1609 and served to defend an already developed civil reality from the levelling influence of a distant political and religious power; while the reparation of war damage initiated urban renewal. Contributors to this process included on the one hand the great administrators – Jan Van Oldenbarneveldt, Jan Pieterszoon Coen – and on the other the 'builders': Lieven De Key, Hendrik De Keyser, Jan Leeghwater, Hendrick Staets. The existing medieval style arrangement was well suited to these specialists, brought up in corporations of citizens and able to execute any sort of civil or military manufacture, but also to consider these problems in scientific terms and to assimilate the visual rules learned from Italy.

Haarlem was besieged in 1572–3 and destroyed by fire in 1576; it was rebuilt immediately afterwards. The municipality entrusted this work to the Stadtfabryk, directed by De Key, a combination technical office and planning authority. At the beginning of the seventeenth century, this project absorbed one-third of the city budget. Based on a survey of the city published in 1578 by Tomas Tomaszoon, this project was largely a renewal of the previous network of roads, canals and lot divisions. The houses and shops of the textile workers were grouped around a long straight canal and De Key also planned several important structures including a fine neighbourhood consisting of groups of homes for old people (1610).

Amsterdam was liberated by William of Orange in 1578 and inherited the economic role of Antwerp. The latter city fell to the Spanish in 1585, but activity was frozen by the Dutch blockade at the mouth of the Scheldt. The great development of Amsterdam began from that date. What had been the surrounding canal was incorporated into the city; the shipyard was built on the city's eastern edge; and in 1593 a semicircle of fortifications was built according to the new rules of Stevin. The central government approved a plan for further enlargement, designed by Staets, in 1607; the necessary land was expropriated and the plan undertaken in 1609. The city's head architect from 1591 to 1621 was De Keyser, who planned and built its major buildings including the Exchange of 1608 and many private houses.

Expansion consisted of three semicircular canals concentric with the fortification of 1593. Each was 25 m wide in order to accommodate four medium-size ships abreast; their lengths were,

61　*Amsterdam: aerial view, showing the three concentric canals built in the seventeenth century (photo: KLM Aerocarto, no. 23509 A).*

62   *An Amsterdam canal (painting by H. P. Schouten, c. 1770).*

respectively, $3\frac{1}{2}$, 4 and $4\frac{1}{2}$ km. Around them ran 11-m loading quays planted with elms, building lots occupying a combined depth of 102 m between canals, and a required internal open space of 48 m. The semicircular composition was broken into a series of straight parallel sections varying from $\frac{1}{2}$ to over 1 km in length, comparable to the court-financed projects in Rome and Paris and Henri IV's canal in the gardens of Fontainebleau (1200 by 40 m). Here, however, the visual rays are obstructed by the trees and the masts of the ships. There are no markers for longitudinal vanishing points, and the houses built on the surrounding lots, governed in their regularity by the parallelism of the canals, are not the standardized backdrops of a uniform vision; instead, each is characterized by a different symmetric façade and occupies a limited axial vision which corresponds to a cross-section of the canal: less than 50 m, as in a medieval square. This urban environment, then, is not a collection of perspective images to be viewed from fixed points, but a continuous series of different elements to be apprehended in motion, a characteristic confirmed

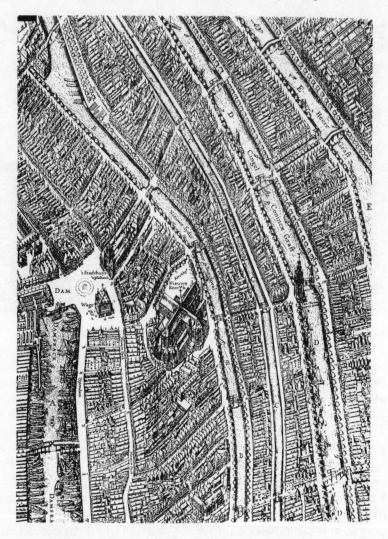

63   *Amsterdam, with the canals in the central area (detail of a view dated 1623, D'Ailly catalogue, no. 117).*

by the countless contemporary images, generally three-quarter or bird's-eye views.

This remarkable organism comprised 25 km of quays frequented by 4,000 ships. Its construction was carried out punctually and in successive stages during the seventeenth century. Employing the 'modern' tools of perspective on an architectural scale together with those of the Classical repertory, financiers and planners succeeded in preserving the principal characters of medieval practice: the rational division of tasks between municipal authorities and private builders, the ability to invent new urban forms independent of regular geometric forms, the close relationship between urban planning and building design, and the co-ordination of space and time. Beginning in the 1630s, a new generation of architects, trained in painting rather than the building trade – Jacob Van Campen, Pieter Post, Salomon De Bray – took on the tasks of designing the specialized buildings, mansions and churches emerging from the urban fabric.

In the course of a century Amsterdam became one of the largest and best-equipped European cities. Population grew from 50,000 in 1612 to 125,000 in 1632, and about 200,000 in the latter half of the century. The outer fortifications, completed at mid-century and then modified according to the 'new Dutch' system of Van Coehorn, enclosed an area of 700 hectares, slightly larger than was customary according to medieval practice. These same methods were successfully applied in other Dutch cities where growth was more moderate: Leiden in 1610 and 1644, Haarlem in 1671; and attempts were made to reproduce them overseas as well: Batavia in 1619, New Amsterdam – later renamed New York by the English conquerors – in 1625, and Cape Town in 1652. These would become great urban centres of the modern world, but their subsequent development followed instead the antithetical model of the Enlightenment architectural grid. The Dutch urban models, perfectly suited to the environment and scale of the Low Countries, were neither exportable nor generalizable.

Dutch technology led the world in many fields – hydraulics, fortifications – while in the figurative arts Holland taught in specific ways how to represent the world spectacle. Together with Rembrandt and Vermeer, the landscape painters – Dujardin, Ruisdael, Koninck, Emanuel de Witte, specialists in the reproduction of scrupulously realistic and emotive scenes, both rural and urban, interior and exterior – communicated to classical European culture the enduring image of the Dutch experience: the penetration of human physiognomy and a sense of the organic unity of the urban and extra-urban setting, made vital by human presence.

These early more or less successful experiments dealt with the application of perspective on an urban scale only in a limited way.

As demonstrated in the case of Holland, these succeeded best when perspective was restricted to a scale only slightly larger than that of a single building.

The task of carrying out fully the confrontation between perspective and the city required a complete re-examination of visual repertory in the context of the new cultural balance. This project was undertaken by artists who began their careers in the 1610s and later: in architecture, Bernini, Borromini, François Mansart, Louis le Vau II, Inigo Jones, and Jacob Van Campen. These individuals cannot be placed in a single group, much less in a 'Baroque' movement somehow reacting to Renaissance classicism. Motivations differed: some sought to conduct new experiments within classicism, while for others, for example in England, classicism itself was an innovation with regard to the existing tradition. It was a movement characterized by personal expression as opposed to the more collective approach of the past. It presented no unified front but rather a plethora of alternative choices, subject to sudden oscillations within a new cultural system in which the term 'art' took on its modern meaning. This array maintained coherence because of the intuitive nature of its approach within the vastly expanded field of classicism; the variety and subtlety of its tools permitted a non-conventional approach to the problems of urban design.

The leading figure in this project was Bernini, who took on the most illustrious and problematic of the historical capitals, Rome, resolving a large number of enduring problems and indicating how the palimpsest of structural fabrics imposed upon this ancient setting might be permanently systemized. In particular, he worked for a lifetime on St Peter's, and managed to achieve a definitive transition across the discontinuity of scale between the gigantic structure of Bramante, Sangallo, Michelangelo and Maderno and the surrounding urban fabric. It was Bernini who achieved the transformation of many architectural ideas suggested over the previous one and a half centuries into coherent elements of a living scenario.

From the time of the Jubilee of 1500, the straight avenue of the Via Alessandrina formed the approach to the Vatican and pointed not at the church, but at the entrance door of the palace. In 1586 the obelisk was erected, and for the first time the axis of the church was marked out in the cityscape, though the new St Peter's of

Bramante and Michelangelo still stood behind the atrium and nave of Constantine's basilica. In 1614, the lengthened church of Maderno faced on to the open space of the piazza, its façade measuring to the gigantic scale imposed by Michelangelo. The palace entrance at the end of the Via Alessandrina was marked by an appropriate avant-corps built in 1618.

The first problem put to the young Bernini was the finishing of the interior of the new church. In 1565 he designed the *baldacchino* for the papal altar, set under the dome and intersecting, but slightly off-centre, the dominant longitudinal axis; between 1637 and 1648 he worked on the interior decoration; and in 1657 he built St Peter's chair in the apse as a concluding backdrop. For the exterior, Bernini first proposed two bell towers on either side of the façade, which proved impossible. Subsequently, following the initiative of Alexander VII, he confronted the problem of the piazza as a whole; between 1656 and 1667 he built the splendid sequence of spaces that co-ordinated the two pre-existing axes, set at a slight angle to each other: the architectural axis linking the church and

64   *Baroque Rome: Piazza San Pietro (photo: Anderson, no. 175).*

the obelisk and the urban axis leading from the city and the Via Alessandrina to the bronze door and, by way of the grand staircase, to the ceremonial and figurative heart of the Vatican, the Sistine Chapel. For the first time, the tools of perspective served to unify, retrospectively, a vast and pre-existing complex. The colossal scale of the mid-sixteenth-century design was gradually attenuated, linked to the normal structural scale, and absorbed into the continuity of the urban setting. Bernini correctly interpreted the attempt to adapt modern Rome to its ancient scale as an uncompleted experiment and accepted the coexistence of monumental and everyday measures; indeed he appropriated this juxtaposition as the primary theme of his work. He consciously ended an epoch and fixed the character of Rome in the European culture that followed: a permanent contrast between the courtly and the common.

Subsequent projects followed Bernini's lead, providing marvellous finishing touches to a stabilized and inimitable urban organism: the piazzetta of Santa Maria della Pace (Pietro da Cortona, 1656); the restoration of the Ponte Sant'Angelo by Bernini himself beginning in 1668; the Spanish Steps (A. Specchi, 1723–6); the Trevi Fountain (N. Salvi, 1732); and Piazza del Popolo, finished by Rainaldi, Bernini (1662–75) and finally Valadier (1784–1816).

Rome's classicism lost its role as a universal model, while remaining an obligatory destination for artists and scholars (the Académie de France was established there by Colbert in 1666) and above all for spiritual pilgrimage. In this latter role it became a permanent trope in literature and the collective imagination, an accumulation of the contrasts between human history and the universal forces that influence it.

The City in Perspective: Urban Transformation from 1650 to 1750

The French artists and writers contemporary with Bernini – Poussin, François Mansart, Corneille, Boileau – embarked upon a new and portentous adventure which had a double theme: the creation of a new, rational and European classicism and the transformation of Paris into a capital befitting the kingdom of France.

65   *Paris: map dated 1550 ('Les Trois Personnages').*

Paris had been seat of the royal court for a century and had
expanded well beyond the medieval walls. On the right bank,
Henri IV and Louis XIII enlarged the fortified circle of walls to
include the Tuileries quarter and the Palais Royal. On the left bank
the Luxembourg residence of Marie de Médicis informed development in the area west of walls of Philippe Auguste. During his
short reign, Henri IV – who admitted deriving pleasure from three
things: war, love and building – initiated a number of projects in
Paris: he built two royal piazzas (one triangular in the Cité, and
one rectangular in the Marais; a third, semicircular piazza was
planned for the high ground by the Temple); he restored the
Louvre and the Tuileries destroyed by civil war, connecting them
with a gallery running along the Seine; and he also planned,
according to Malherbe, to complete the Cour-Carrée and connect
the two palaces along a line to the north as well, following the rue
Saint-Honoré, which required the demolition of the intervening
quarter. The first of these programmes was completed by Louis
XIV, the second by Napoleon III.

Henri IV also initiated – in the field of construction as else-where – the reorganization of the administrative apparatus which served as the basis for absolute monarchy. Yet while the Dutch provincial governments undertook tasks complementary to those of private builders (designing, urbanizing and reselling the building areas), the French apparatus took up only projects and specula-tions already begun and was not capable of rationalizing a city undergoing such rapid and considerable growth: the population of about 200,000 at the end of the sixteenth century grew to 415,000 in 1637. The rulers preferred to reside outside the city – Henri IV in Saint-Germain, Marie de Médicis in the Palais du Luxem-bourg – and in a sense the court stood in opposition to the city; while power resided at court, the realm of public opinion was the city. This heterogeneous collectivity, linked to the authority of the state but at the same time impervious to its logic, was characterized by an indefinable physical form, built on an inadequate medieval plan and overloaded with population and buildings. This preca-rious equilibrium hid and aggravated the political and social contradictions of the nation.

Decisive cultural choices were made in the period between the deaths of Louis XIII and Richelieu (1643–4) and the assumption of power by Louis XIV (1661). A partial but significant antagonism endured between culture and power in artistic and literary circles. The experiences of Poussin – renowned but permanently exiled in Rome – and François Mansart – marginalized in favour of Lemer-cier – resemble those of Corneille, Descartes and Pascal. The world of culture dispassionately looked after its own interests and worked for a plurality of public and private patrons, all competing among themselves.

In the embellishment of physical settings many specialized contributions were combined, and encountered the problems of personal and social behaviour. Around mid-century the need to create total environments came to the fore; their realization required the combined efforts of architecture, figurative art and an environmental planning as yet unnamed. We have already dis-cussed the design of Piazza San Pietro in Rome, which expanded the Italian architectural experience to an urban scale. There appeared in France in those same years, and not by coincidence, the first similarly ambitious architectural setting: the Château de Vaux, built between 1656 and 1660 by Le Vau, Le Nôtre and Le Brun for the wealthy superintendent of finances, Nicolas Fouquet.

66 *Vaux: overhead aerial view of the park (photo: Institut Géographique National, no. 27).*

Le Vau, descended from a line of builders, was the preferred architect of the financiers of the period. Le Nôtre and Le Brun studied together in the *atelier* of Vouet. Le Nôtre inherited from his father the position of gardener of the Tuileries in 1637 and became the general superintendent of construction in 1656. Le Brun was in Rome from 1642 to 1647, where he associated with Poussin, and subsequently specialized in interior decoration. The three collaborated on the Vaux project, commanding a large force of workers and undertaking to control an entire landscape, attending to details of both topographical and decorative scale.

The control of a single artist like Bernini, responsible for the visual scenario on all scales, was replaced by a collective effort in which the garden specialist not the architect dominated; for the principal 'structure' at Vaux is the garden designed by Le Nôtre, which defines the place and character of the other elements of the whole. Renaissance gardens generally extended the structural axes of symmetry without exceeding the normal limits of architectural space, a few hundred metres, or seeking to compete with the surrounding natural spaces. The garden at Vaux, instead, occupies a space that is still limited, a hollow measuring about 1 by 2 km, carved out of a woody plateau, but large enough to fill the visual plain as far as a border which serves as an infinite horizon.

The château breaks up the longitudinal axis and separates two unequal environments: the entrance courtyard around which the services were centred, and the garden reserved for the nobility. The variegated façade opening on to the garden can be seen from afar and dominates a complex and undulating setting of terraces which terminate in a play of water. At the lowest elevation there stretches an orthogonal canal which marks out the transverse axis and compensates for the incline of the terrain by means of its differently spaced end-points.

It is a symmetric composition which is gradually modified and indeed led astray in the failed attempt to establish continuity with the asymmetric physical setting in which it is placed. While Renaissance gardens respected and even emphasized the subordinate status of architecture with respect to the natural world, the garden at Vaux included the natural backdrop and, using the tools of architecture, pursued its scenic dimensions to the limits of visual perception. It was a case of art attempting to explore on its own account the new ideas of practical infinity and forcing the usual frontiers of perspective to this end.

Successive events clarified the importance of this innovation. On 17 August 1661 Fouquet invited the king and his court to an evening which included a dinner prepared by Vatel; a ballet composed by Molière, directed by Le Brun and with music by Lully; and a show of fireworks in the garden. Three weeks later Colbert had the superintendent arrested, confiscated his wealth and had the artists from Vaux put in the king's service. Colbert had in mind above all the systemization of Paris, while Louis XIV began the enlargement of Versailles. These turned out to be competing projects in a society where each required a questionable use of public money.

In a famous letter of 1663 Colbert went so far as to criticize Louis XIV because he preferred to stay in Versailles for the sake of diversion while he should instead be in Paris for the sake of glory. For once Colbert overlooked the 'difficultés à l'exécution' which in a constructed setting like that of Paris were prohibitive. Reconstruction of the Louvre quadrangle, on which Bernini collaborated between 1664 and 1665, was a drawn-out affair; the surrounding projects – the square in front of the east façade, connection with the Tuileries – lacked in both administrative and financial means. The open countryside of Versailles provided instead a setting in which the resources of absolutism were sufficient to accomplish the large-scale modifications required by that absolutism for its own celebration. Fields, trees, pools of water and statues were put in order, as there were neither buildings nor people to undergo this treatment. In 1682 the entire royal court was moved into this inanimate setting and only there found an appropriate physical environment. 'There are more statues in his palace gardens than there are citizens in a large town'[2] was the comment of Montesquieu's Usbek in 1721 after completion of Louis XIV's projects.

At Versailles, Le Nôtre repeated the experiment conducted at Vaux and expanded it to the limits of perception. Three large avenues converged before the palace and around these grew an entire city. Behind the palace a vast woodland was disciplined according to the symmetry of the principal building. This was accomplished by means of two canals forming a cross which defined the Cartesian co-ordinates of the composition and also reflected the setting sun. Repeatedly expanded, the palace attained proportions appropriate to its surroundings only after 1677 when Hardouin-Mansart transformed it into a vast but compact omega-shaped form. From a distance, Le Vau's work on the façade, derived from Bernini's projects for the Louvre, disappears, and one perceives only the general inflection of the structure's mass. The view, coming from Paris, is of the building's concavity, which reveals at its centre the emergent remains of the original castle containing the royal apartments. From the garden, the central salient defines the main perspective axis, and projects slightly if viewed from below; from further away, however, it blends into a uniform block that holds back and in some ways contains the immense expanse of the garden. The *piano nobile* of the central

67   *Versailles: the Grand Canal from the Bassin de Latone (photo: Benevolo).*

section contains the hall of mirrors which serves to display the magnificent garden as well as its reflection in the mirrors of the back wall.

The construction project of Versailles, which employed 35,000 workers in 1685, was the largest in Europe for non-military purposes since Roman times. Le Nôtre, Le Brun and Hardouin-Mansart directed thousands of specialized artists in all manner of detailed work. At the same time as work proceeded on Versailles, the three planners were fitting out the king's retreat at Marly and, for other members of the court, the residences of Saint-Cloud, Chantilly, Sceaux, Meudon and Clagny. Paris itself underwent developments modelled after these gardens. The medieval centre received only minor modifications by the insertion of several isolated architectural elements (Place Vendôme and Place des Victoires), but the right-bank arc of fortifications was transformed into a belt of *grands boulevards*, while straight tree-lined roads converged on the ancient gates and created a discontinuous suburb of parks and bourgeois homes.

This open city and its monuments of greenery, not requiring fortifications because the kingdom was protected by a line of fortresses along the frontier, was new and surprising. Contemporary commentary expressed both admiration and hostility: Boileau described it as a land of plenty where a wealthy man could go to the countryside without leaving the city;[3] La Bruyère employed a description of the Chantilly garden as an introduction to reflections on the ordered cosmos.[4] The new manipulation of green spaces, however, was criticized in moral terms (Bussy-Rabutin described it as forcing the land into an unnatural form)[5] and the money spent considered excessive, though it was only a small fraction of that spent on wars.

Building projects were often carried out by military units and so were subject to the unexpected developments of war. As a result, the regularity achieved in the artificial enclosures of Le Nôtre's gardens is lacking in the overall territorial design, and betrays a serious lack of financial and organizational means. For the fountains of Versailles there was never sufficient water so that the fountain workers had to run them in turn as the king made his way through the *petit parc*; subsequently a machine to pump water from the Seine at Marly was installed, water was brought from the highlands of Saclay, and plans were made to bring it from the Eure as well. Huge works for the latter project were interrupted in 1688. The palace housed an incredible intermingling of about 10,000 members of the court; from time to time, overwhelmed by the accumulation of filth, the king and his court were sent to 'take air' at Marly or elsewhere so that the work of cleaning could be accomplished. The calculated, severe, detached architectural setting of Le Nôtre and Hardouin-Mansart served as a backdrop to this promiscuous society. Functional disorder was disguised by the structural façades; daily events were lost in the vast external and internal spaces. Visual decorum stood in conscious opposition to these occurrences, presenting a conventional image of regality and prestige which would endure as exemplary models through time and space.

French style in art, literature and manners, developed during the *grand siècle*, stood as models from the late seventeenth century on, so that even forms inherited from Classical antiquity and Europe in general were interpreted through the filter of French classicism. In almost all capitals the court divided its residence between an

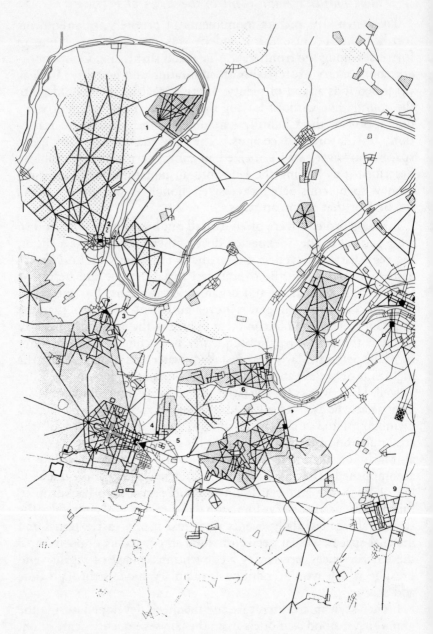

68   Paris and its environs, with the grands boulevards *and gardens, in the first half of the eighteenth century. Baroque areas (in heavy outline) are superimposed on the medieval layout, but the two do not blend.*

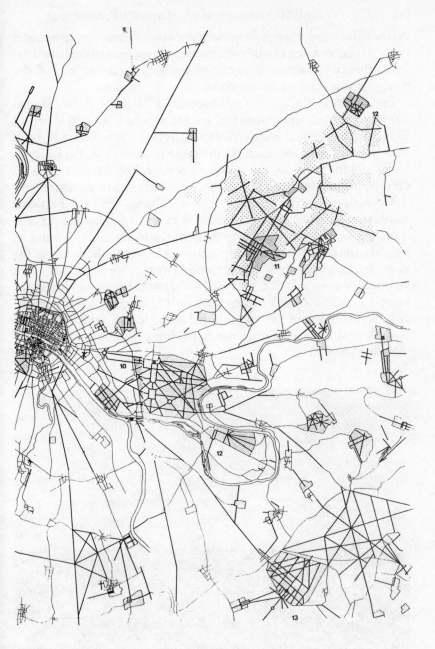

(1) Maisons; (2) Saint-Germain; (3) Marly; (4) Versailles; (5) Clagny; (6) Saint-Cloud; (7) Bois de Boulogne; (8) Meudon; (9) Sceaux; (10) Vincennes; (11) Livry; (12) Saint-Maur; (13) Gros Bois.

urban palace and a series of suburban parks. Resources invested in these parks, and the notable architectural results accomplished far from the city, were compensated by a general neglect of the medieval installations in the cities.

In Madrid Philip V sponsored a series of utilitarian works – bridges, aqueducts and fountains – and, after the fire of 1734, the new royal palace designed by Juvara and slowly built over the following decades. At the same time he took Versailles as his model for work on the country residences of Aranjuez and La Granja, located far from the city and not affecting its development.

Vienna became the capital of the Habsburgs after the Battle of Kahlenberg in 1683 and was rebuilt with special defensive precautions. An open ½-km-wide strip isolated the medieval centre and its fortifications. The surrounding settlements were rebuilt along the radial roads and defended by a second circle of fortifications and a second open strip of 200 metres. Fischer von Erlach, architect for Joseph I and Charles VI from 1690 to 1723, employed a particularly stylistic design for the imperial architecture, which included both the royal palace within the city (Hofburg) and that outside it (Schönbrunn).

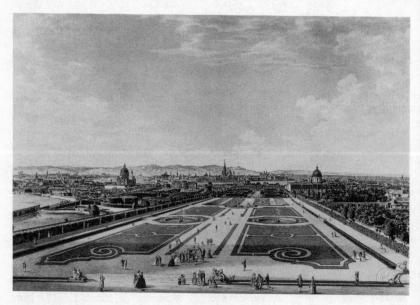

69   *Vienna from the Belvedere Gardens (photo: Albertina, no. 620–70).*

Max Emanuel of Bavaria, exiled in Paris from 1704 to 1715, brought François Girard with him to Munich. The latter designed the two parks of Nymphenburg and Schlessheim and then, for the archbishop of Cologne, that of Brühl. The urban organism and parks were combined with pleasing results in Berlin (expanded several times beginning in 1640), Dresden (rebuilt after the fire of 1685) and Würzburg (transformed from a bourgeois city to the residence of the prince-bishops after 1714). In Karlsruhe, the new capital founded by the margrave of Durlach in 1715, a single radiating design converging on the palace, commands both the park and the city.

The new Russian capital of St Petersburg, founded in 1703 by Peter the Great on the Baltic estuary of the River Neva, presents still another case. For the first decade it was a fortified outpost where 100,000 prisoners were employed as workers, and to which court dignitaries were persuaded to move only by force. In 1712 the tsar attempted to impose a regular design, bringing Schlüter from Berlin and Le Blond from Paris, but failed. After his death, the city grew by partial additions around a radiating pattern of three roads converging towards the Admiralty and traced out in 1730. It maintained a refined and fascinating character: a mosaic of

70 *St Petersburg; the Winter Palace in snowy weather (eighteenth-century engraving).*

buildings and gardens in a vast area out of which emerge the polychrome monuments built by Rastrelli for Elizabeth around the mid-eighteenth century. The great parks of Peterhof, Tsarskoe Selo and Oranienbaum developed in the surrounding area.

Everywhere French *grand goût* (good taste) stood as a sign of modernity. Even the emperor of China employed two Jesuit missionaries to create a small European garden in the park of his summer palace. The guiding thread of these experiments was the application of perspective to a series of different physical settings, each presumably capable of conformity to Classical visual rules. The often exaggerated and paradoxical tension characteristic of the end-product derived from the risk inherent in this combination, and above all from the forcing of dimensions to the limits of perception.

Given normal topographical conditions, a perspective axis can be extended to about 3 km. This is the distance from the Château de Versailles to the small elevation at the end of the *grand canal* that serves as an infinite backdrop. Greater distances require greater changes in altitude in order to be visible.

In Kassel, the landgrave of Hesse-Nassau built, starting in 1700, the Wilhelmshohe park on the peak of a mountain and erected there an enlarged reproduction of the Farnese *Hercules*. A waterfall descends from this point in line with the city palace. The visual axis does not follow the ground but runs through the air for $7\frac{1}{2}$ km with a change of altitude of 400 m.

In Turin, Victor Amadeus II had a new straight boulevard built to Rivoli in 1712, where the suburban royal palace was under construction. Juvara arrived in 1714 and planned the Superga basilica. He had the brilliant idea of placing it in line with this boulevard on the hill above the opposite bank of the Po. In this way a conventional road cut out a perspective of $19\frac{1}{2}$ km, descending over 100 m from Rivoli to Turin and then soaring in the air up to the dome set on a woody hill 430 m above. The Rivoli castle and its great stairways stand out as the arrival point of the opposite view. The two monuments mark out the narrow stretch between the two mountain chains, the Alps and the Apennines, which enclose Turin and across which is stretched a fragile and perilous visual cord. It is the longest architectural display in the world, using the tools of perspective and, in addition, taking into account the clarity of the air and the compactness of the physical setting.

These latter two considerations no longer apply, but the daring calculation is in some ways still evident in the confused setting of the present.

The Bourbon Charles III began the suburban residence of Caserta in 1752. The road from Naples, following the Roman subdivision of the countryside, bends slightly to the east at a certain point and heads towards a spur of Monte San Leucio, $6\frac{1}{2}$ km away and 250 m higher. The final stretch of the road, the royal palace and the garden are all aligned along this axis and take as their vanishing point the waterfall coming down the mountain. The adjacent urban nucleus was set out according to this same orientation.

These extraordinary constructions concluded, on the eve of the Enlightenment, the great experiment of perspective design, an experiment which responded to the aspirations and illusions of the Baroque age without losing contact with direct visual experience or crossing over into the realm of utopia. The demand for geometric regularity encountered a network of urban settlements dating from the late Middle Ages and only partially capable of modification. It was in the great not yet urbanized settings that perspective design enjoyed its boldest application. Out of these experiments derived the tension and prominence of its greatest productions: the world of Versailles closed within an artificial horizon, the spider's thread spun between Rivoli and Superga, the carefully spaced setting of water, parks and monuments under the arctic sky of St Petersburg.

When the geometric representation of the universe moved, during the Enlightenment, into the realm of abstraction and lost contact with physical perception, this earlier approach to the physical setting was eclipsed and its daring devices forgotten. Following generations would extract a simplified version, lacking the elements of exaggeration and paradox; it was employed in Washington, in nineteenth-century Paris, in Berlin, Chicago and New Delhi in order to dignify centres of political and economic power.

Departure from Perspective: The English Experience

After the Restoration of 1660, Charles II encouraged the re-establishment of contacts with continental Europe: a link to the

Dutch classicism of Van Campen and Post was achieved by way of Hugh May, keeper of the privy purse, who had been exiled to Amsterdam together with the Duke of Buckingham; the *grand goût* of French gardens was brought by André and Gabriel Mollet, sons of Le Nôtre's teacher Claude Mollet and employed by Charles in 1661. The royal structures of Whitehall, Hampton Court and Greenwich were built according to these imported models.

The great London fire of 1666 presented an opportunity, unique in Europe, for the large-scale reconstruction of a great city according to 'modern' design. The eight innovative projects of Wren, Hooke, Evelyn, Knight and Newcourt proved unworkable, as the destruction of the fire failed to eliminate the economic and administrative obstacles encountered in other European capitals: a lack of co-ordination between public and private interests and the uncertainty of financial and legal instruments. However, the response of English planners to these difficulties was practical and unprejudiced. Their architectural ability was not based upon an artistic education, but on other sorts of preparation: Wren and Hooke were fellows of the Royal Society for Improving Natural Knowledge by Experiments, Evelyn was a wealthy dilettante, and Knight was a military man. Nor did their experience include immersion in the rules of Renaissance perspective which accentuated the continental confrontation with the difficulties of urban planning and led to the search for alternative settings, outside the cities, for the application of perspective design.

The 1667 Act for Rebuilding the City of London reaffirmed the previous cadastral design with several improvements: the widening of streets, the canalization of rivers and the introduction of building regulations. Within this rigid canvas, modern planning found a more limited scope: public buildings like Jerman's Stock Exchange, Mills's Guildhall of the City Corporation, and the churches of Wren, Archer and Gibbs; the subdivision of suburban terrain from which emerged the symmetrical residential areas of Bloomsbury Square (1661), Grosvenor Square (1695), Cavendish Square (1717), Berkeley Square (1730), Bedford Square (1775) and Russell Square (1800); the two new bridges of Westminster (1751) and Blackfriars (1760) across the Thames; the royal parks: Hyde Park, opened to the public in 1640 and given an artificial lake in 1830, St James's Park with Charles II's straight avenue, and Pall

Mall; and the promenades created by private initiative: Vauxhall Gardens and Ranelagh Gardens with the covered rotunda of 1741.

These medium-scale experiments, freely arranged side by side, formed an open and continuous narrative. Each responded to a regular and easily read design, but the combination escaped simple definition. Meanwhile, the city grew out of all measure, reaching a million inhabitants at the end of the eighteenth century. The concave shape of the terrain, sloping down to the Thames, presented the confusing image of this immense body as a series of overlapping emergent forms, captured in the cityscapes painted by Canaletto in the mid-eighteenth century and in Wordsworth's description from the early nineteenth:

> Ships, towers, domes, theatres, and temples lie
> Open unto the fields and to the sky,
> All bright and glittering in the smokeless air.[6]

The vast size of the metropolis revealed itself in the enormous amount of vehicular and pedestrian traffic, inspiring this epic comment by John Gay:

> Who can recount the coach's various harms,
> The legs disjointed and the broken arms?[7]

In the more usual dimensions of the smaller English cities, this method of putting together the urban setting produced results of extraordinary quality: the squares and crescents built by the Woods in Bath between 1727 and 1770, and the expansions in Edinburgh after the competition of 1767, all liberal juxtapositions of symmetrical forms consciously adapted to the irregularity of the rolling terrain.

Meanwhile, perspective regularity was consciously abandoned in the English gardens of the first half of the eighteenth century, a change heralded in theoretical debate. Gardens built at the end of the seventeenth century and in the early eighteenth – Badminton (1682), Chatsworth (1685) and Melbourne Hall (1704), reproduced in Knyff and Kip's *Le Nouveau Théâtre de la Grand Bretagne* of 1714[8] – followed French courtly models, but encountered a literary movement already headed in the opposite direction. Shaftesbury in 1709, Addison in 1712 and Pope in 1713 all criticized the enforcement of regular patterns on landscape and vegetation. Pope himself personally designed the garden of his home in Twicken-

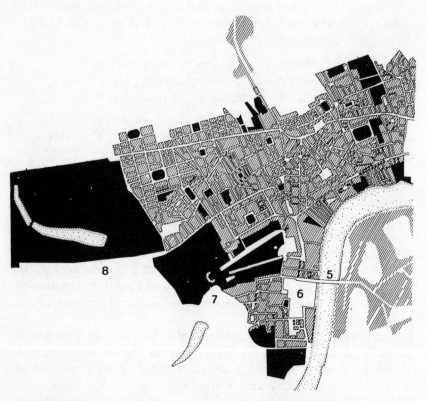

71 London in the eighteenth century, showing the layout of the periphery: (1) the City; (2) Tower of London; (3) London Bridge; (4) Blackfriars Bridge; (5) Westminster Bridge; (6) Westminster; (7) St James's Park; (8) Hyde Park. Green areas are shown in black.

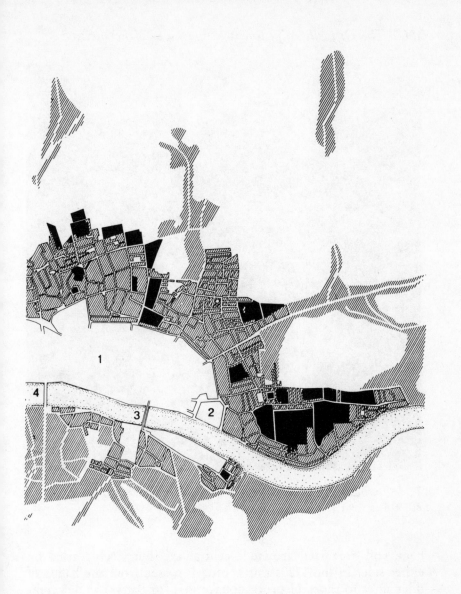

72   *Stourhead: aerial view of the grounds (photo: Aerofilms Ltd, no. 801916).*

ham, still organized around a central axis but freely varied on either side. In the 1720s this approach passed from the hands of dilettantes to those of professionals: in 1726 Batty Langley published his *New Principles of Gardening*,[9] and in 1729 William Kent took on the garden of Chiswick for Lord Burlington. Lancelot Brown, originally assistant to Kent at Stowe, later achieved enormous personal success, completing more than 100 projects including Warwick Castle, Chatsworth and Blenheim; it is said that he turned down a job in Ireland claiming that he had not yet finished with England.

Langley and Kent were trained in figurative art, while Brown's technical apprenticeship allowed him to take a detached view of stylistic choices and so make the great leap: the abandonment of all reference to Cartesian geometry and the direct imitation of the irregularity of nature. There is a paradox at the crux of this experiment: just as with the great continental perspective projects, Brown had to 'force nature' like Le Nôtre, flattening hills, hollowing out valleys and stream beds, planting and uprooting trees, all so that the final result appeared natural. The hierarchy of visual reference points, however, was lost and the garden opened to an infinity of possible paths of exploration lacking either start or finish. Architecture no longer served to regulate the overall composition, and individual buildings appeared as isolated objects in the landscape with an entirely new and surprising effect. Just beyond their thresholds the customary axes and spatial measures ended and the unexplorable complexity of the natural world reigned.

These settings realized the general aesthetic ideals of the mid-eighteenth century: the 'waving line of beauty' proposed by Hogarth in 1745;[10] Burke's *Philosophical Enquiry into the Origin of our Ideas of the Sublime and the Beautiful* of 1756;[11] Horace Walpole's historical recounting in his essay on *The History of Modern Taste in Gardening* (1770).[12]. Accompanied by these theoretical elaborations, the 'English Garden' spread throughout Europe in the latter half of the century: Louis XV hired the Englishman Richard to design the garden of the Petit Trianon at Versailles; Philippe d'Orléans built the Parc Monceau in Paris; the Duke of Anhalt built the Wörlitz Park in Dessau; and Prince Karl August built with the help of Goethe the park at Weimar. It was in fact Goethe who, describing the Dessau park in a letter to Frau von Stein in 1778, captured with special perceptiveness the nature of this new landscape: 'The sight of a hill does not incline us toward a specific goal; instead we continue to amble without asking where we have arrived or where we are going.'[13] This concept of an escape into nature reappears insistently in the literature of the day, from Rousseau's *Nouvelle Héloïse* (1761) to Goethe's *Wahlverwandtschaften* (1809), and finds its origin in a fascination with untamed nature, not disturbed by man. The search for a three-dimensional setting not conforming to geometric laws was satisfied in the mountains. Mont Blanc was first climbed in 1786, because it was there (to borrow a later phrase), and signalled the beginning of modern mountaineering.

The English garden was poised between the 'picturesque' tradition and the new sensibility for nature. Its curvilinear designs were the most sophisticated product of the eighteenth-century taste for asymmetrical ornamentation in rockery, and also represented an emotional recollection of the Neolithic freedom of movement in an infinite space. The appearance of architectural elements in this context – codified microcosms in an infinitely variable macrocosmic setting – took on a troubling and entirely new intensity.

The same individuals who brought about this change in gardening design also accomplished the demotion of classicism from its role as the required language of architecture, and the revival of a Gothic alternative. Following the isolated Gothic additions of Wren and Hawksmoor at Oxford, William Kent constructed a Gothic façade at Hampton Court for Robert Walpole in the courtyard facing the Tudor room (1738). In 1742 Batty Langley published a handbook on Gothic style. Subsequently, a number of Gothic homes were built for scholars and connoisseurs including Horace Walpole's Strawberry Hill at Twickenham (1749–77) and William Beckford's Fonthill Abbey (1796). The Gothic revival became a European movement in the first decades of the nineteenth century; and in 1807 Chateaubriand restored his residence at Vallée-aux-Loups in Gothic style.

The three innovations described above – the uncoupling of building composition from the composition of the urban scale, the design of external spaces without reference to the rules of perspective, and the substitution of Gothic for Classical style – attacked the most fundamental tenets of Renaissance aesthetic/visual culture: the revival of the Gothic repertory disavowed the universal value of the normalized elements taken from Classical antiquity; the naturalistic garden signalled the abandonment of spatial representation according to the Cartesian axes and extended the rejection of symmetry, till then attempted only on the small scale of ornamentation, to a large scale. The separation of urban planning from building design eliminated the continuity of architectural choices on varying scales and brought into being a new sort of urban continuum, impervious to the traditional forms of perception and control.

In the attempt to complete the urban system, European culture used up its traditional tools and so prepared the way for a radical change in the sort of choices that would be made. In the period that followed, these choices, together with technological and economic developments, transformed the physical setting produced in the preceding centuries. Meanwhile, on the threshold of this transformation, there was a lingering over the existing urban and rural landscapes where the contributions of a long history found for the last time a measure of harmonious integration; the characteristics of this setting were reproduced, popularized, discussed and in some ways bidden farewell.

The late seventeenth-century Venetian, English and Dutch landscape paintings, etchings, guidebooks, and travel literature reveal a widespread interest in the physical setting of Europe and the world as a whole. In the period of great changes at the end of the eighteenth century and the beginning of the nineteenth, the habit of looking around oneself and expanding the visual field to the surrounding landscape formed the frame of events, whether reassuring or elusive, like the sky over the Battle of Austerlitz described by Tolstoy. For us, this enormous mass of images and observations documents a balanced landscape that has been in large part destroyed and so no longer reassures. The ordered European setting of the last pre-industrial phase will serve as a point of reference and an incentive for the task that awaits us: to remedy the disequilibria of recent transformations and so recapture, if only partially, the balance that has been lost.

6

The Industrial City

Urban Revolution

Europe was created by ten centuries of political, economic and cultural events to which it is linked by a complex system of reciprocal causality. At the end of the eighteenth century a number of these events passed a critical threshold, acquiring revolutionary status and plunging Europe into crisis. The relevant transformations included institutional changes, the application of scientific progress to productive technology, and the combination of economic and demographic growth.

The factors which had an impact on the architectural setting can be summed up as follows:

(1) The processes of the Industrial Revolution, including population increase, increased industrial production, and the mechanization of productive systems, began in England in the mid-eighteenth century and then spread at varying speeds to the other European states; these processes altered, for the first time since the thirteenth century, the quantitative and qualitative dimensions of the European urban system.

Population increase, combined with migration transfers from the countryside to the city, fuelled rapid urban growth. London passed the one-million mark at the end of the eighteenth century and reached 2,500,000 by 1851, exceeding all other cities, ancient or modern. An industrial city like Manchester grew from 12,000 inhabitants in 1760 to 400,000 in the mid-nineteenth century. At the same time, land was cultivated according to a new organization and on a capitalist basis; new roads, canals and, after 1830, railways were built. Industry concentrated first along the avenues of water transport and then around the coalmining centres, radically transforming vast sections of countryside. Sailing-ships were gradually replaced by steamships, and the ports adapted accordingly.

These material changes were exaggerated and distorted by the impression of novelty that dominated both popular and educated imagination. The 'new' was often interpreted in extreme terms, positive or negative, and so either enthusiastically embraced or rejected. Dickens's retrospective judgement from the opening of *A Tale of Two Cities* (1859) stands as a general comment:

> It was the best of times, it was the worst of times, it was the age of wisdom, it was the age of foolishness, it was the epoch of belief, it was the epoch of incredulity, it was the season of Light, it was the season of Darkness, it was the spring of hope, it was the winter of despair, we had everything before us, we had nothing before us, we were all going direct to Heaven, we were all going direct the other way – in short, the period was so far like the present period, that some of its noisiest authorities insisted on its being received, for good or for evil, in the superlative degree of comparison only.[1]

(2) Re-examination of the European cultural legacy, beginning with the great inventory compiled in the *Encyclopédie* of Diderot and d'Alembert (1751–65), was conducted by the light of reason, identifying a unique objective order in all aspects of reality.

This method, already applied successfully in the area of scientific and technological research, invaded the sphere of individual and collective relationships, disturbing the usual divisions between the various realms of experience. In his 1776 essay on *The Wealth of Nations*, Adam Smith proposed a natural order of economic relationships, comparable to those revealed by Lavoisier in the physical sciences. Personal sentiments, described with great emotional empathy by Goethe in his *Sorrows of Young Werther* of 1774, analysed with detachment and irony by Laclos in his *Liaisons dangereuses* of 1782, and violated by the physiological rage of the accounts of the Marquis de Sade which appeared between 1791 and 1796, came to the fore alike in imagination and in reality. Reappraisal of this sort led to the inclusion of a vast array of intellectual and emotional themes in the area of artistic representation and the explosion of traditional divisions.

In the field of visual culture, the two fundamental elements of the Renaissance tradition – perspective regularity and conformity to Classical models – were individually dissected and plunged into crisis.

Progress in mathematics, optics and the technology of instruments contributed to the sciences of geodesy and cartography, making possible the precise representation of terrestrial surfaces in any scale. The Cassini family began publication in 1750 of a great map of France, completed in 1815. The first precise measurements of long distances were made in that same year, using the same technology which enabled Lalande and Lacaille to measure the lunar parallax. The entire planet earth became an object of observation. Polar expeditions between 1736 and 1774 revealed that the earth was a spheroid slightly flattened at the poles. Measurement of the Paris meridian, called for by the Constituent Assembly in 1791 and carried out between 1792 and 1798, provided by its division a new standard of measure, the metre, made obligatory in France in 1801 and gradually adopted in other countries. As already mentioned, after 1785 the subdivision of new territories in the United States was made according to a grid along lines of latitude and longitude.

Progress of this sort upset the previously existing relationship between geometric representation and the world of immediate sensations. Perspective, which dealt with the control of visible forms, was absorbed into the descriptive geometry of Monge, which indiscriminately represented all of three-dimensional space in two dimensions. The metre, derived from an astronomical measurement, substituted for traditional units linked to the human body – the yard, the foot, the inch – and spatial measurement lost its relationship to human movement. The various scales of planning flowed together into an unlimited mental dimension within which the products of technology took shape separately and without the constraint of a uniform visual filter.

In this same spirit the great models of antiquity were verified using the precise tools of archaeology and art history. The systematic excavations of Herculaneum began in 1711, of Hadrian's Villa at Tivoli in 1729, and of Pompeii in 1748. The first public museums were opened at the Campidoglio in Rome in 1732, at the Vatican in 1739 and in London in 1759. Precise drawings of Greek monuments appeared for the first time[2] and Stuart built the

first correct copy of a Doric temple at Hagley in 1758. Winckelmann's *History of Ancient Art* appeared in 1764.[3] Classicism, the
basis of European taste over the previous three centuries, became a
specific and debated programme – Neoclassicism – competing
with Neogothic and all the other styles of the past that historians
were rapidly studying and classifying. A plurality of alternative
rules replaced a single stylistic standard, rules that required
justification by means of external political, ideological and moral
arguments.

All this changed the framework for decisions in the world of
visual forms, but also the role of the visual in culture and everyday
life. The buildingscape of late eighteenth-century Europe, in which
the contributions of the past found for the last time a measure of
harmony and peace, no longer stood at the forefront of research
and innovation. It became a coherent but generic background,
where nothing more of importance would take place, as new
experimentation had moved on to other fields.

The relationship between late eighteenth-century revolutionary
movements and Neoclassicism was of a similar nature, though still
more significant is the comparison between that which took place
in the fine arts – architecture, sculpture, applied arts – and in
music. Just when the European artistic lingua franca split off in
several opposed and extreme directions, there came into existence a
unified musical culture, later called 'Classical', which, both balanced and equilibrating, followed an alternative and harmonious
path. While literary and artistic movements replaced one another
with frightening speed, Viennese classicism created a stable and
organically structured musical universe which guarded the cultural
continuity of a society undergoing rapid change. Its function as
inspiration, public entertainment and private consolation was
comparable to that of the Renaissance visual culture of the fifteenth
and sixteenth centuries, and served to counterbalance contemporary images of the urban environment, the domestic setting and the
new forces of production. The early nineteenth-century crisis of
authenticity, the contentious reaction in the latter half of the
century and the avant-garde movements around the turn of the
twentieth century form a sequence of events that are explicable and
comprehensible if we keep in mind this other area of intellectual
and sentimental refuge which filled public and private life in this
same period.

To sum up: on the one hand art took on the task of communicating emotion and organizing the 'language of the heart'; on the other the urban setting was cut off from this process. Art was stripped from the city and became an experience specific to certain spaces, to be enjoyed during leisure time. Emotion separated from the city stood exposed and vulnerable. The city separated from emotion remained an interchangeable backdrop, capable of proving alien and hostile.

(3)   The coherence of architectural and urban planning relied on institutional mechanisms which were challenged by enlightened criticism and revolution in the late eighteenth century.

The setting of cities, towns, castles, parks, roads, canals, bridges, cultivated plots, workshops, mines, ports and military works was largely formed in the last centuries of the Middle Ages. The new visual culture of the Renaissance and Baroque periods modified, expanded and refined this setting by means of a series of difficulties and conflicts discussed in the two preceding chapters. Occasionally the limits of cultural rules were strained. All, however, remained within an institutional and social continuum retrospectively identified as *ancien régime*.

Diversity of political, religious and economic situations did not bring into question the double responsibility, public and private, on which every long-term modification of the buildingscape depended. For each particular project there was a *dominus*, but above him stood a *dominus eminens*, responsible in a more general sense, who commanded the former without negating his sphere of autonomy. When the two roles coincided, in the absolute prince, his omnipotence, though given rhetorical prominence, was in fact limited by other rival institutions and above all by the precariousness of economic resources; no European monarch possessed the means to create, destroy or modify cities after the fashion of an Asian despot. The organic quality of structural forms which made up the unified and multiform façade of eighteenth-century Europe derived from this balance of prerogatives, always swaying but never falling one way or the other.

The attenuation of control from above with respect to that of private initiative becomes more evident in more recent monumental projects. In Paris, Louis XIV had the building façades of the Place Vendôme constructed, and the statue of the king was inaugurated in 1699; it stood at the centre of an architectural screen

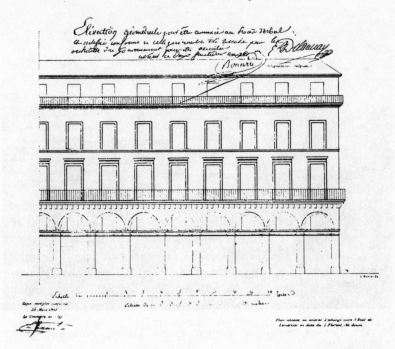

73 *Uniform design for the façades of buildings in the rue de Rivoli,
Paris, by Percier and Fontaine, 1806.*

behind which the buildings were yet to be constructed. In the rue
Royale, the city administration took on the task of building the
façades on the lots of others and then selling these to the owners at
a pre-established price while paying them rent from 1757 for
occupation of the land. In the rue de Rivoli the structures were
constructed by many different builders, but each was obliged to
employ the same design for the façade provided by Percier and
Fontaine in 1806.

Both the revolutions and reforms of the late eighteenth and early
nineteenth centuries undermined the sort of collective responsibility that had traditionally governed projects of this sort. New legal
ordinances regulated the spheres of private property and private
initiative and established that public authorities could intervene
only according to a fixed and accurately defined procedure. In the
area of property, notarized acts and land registers set the relevant
limits, and these were the basis of ownership and taxation as well.

74   An English industrial district: Colne Valley, Yorkshire (photo:
Yorkshire Post, *Leeds).*

Building and land-use decisions were specifically the province of
property owners, whether public or private.

All the regulations, customs and other mechanisms that me-
diated between the individual and the state with regard to the
construction and traditional management of the buildingscape
were dismantled, all at once as in France, or else gradually as in
England. Property initiatives conformed to the same code as other
economic initiatives, subject to the laws of the market-place and
freed of the intervention of public administrations. Attempts at
intervention of the latter sort were considered obstructions, useless
hangovers from the past to be eliminated. Adam Smith urged
governments to divest themselves of property holdings.

This tendency revealed itself in both revolutionary and reformist
legislation, and at just the time when cities were growing and being
transformed in a way they had not since the thirteenth century.
Regulation waned while the changes needing regulation increased.
Out of this fatal combination erupted the chaotic settings

described by the authors of the first half of the nineteenth century (Chadwick and Engels in England, Blanc and Villermé in France)[4]: huge suburbs of new and precarious houses were mixed together with factories and became uninhabitable for lack of public space and basic sanitary services (running water, sewage, rubbish disposal). Heinrich Heine, coming to London from a still traditional Germany in 1828, recorded this impression:

> I have seen the greatest wonder which the world can show to the astonished spirit; I have seen it, and am still astonished; and still there remains fixed in my memory the stone forest of houses, and amid them the rushing stream of faces of living men with all their motley passions, all their terrible impulses of love, of hunger, and of hatred . . . This downright earnestness of all things, this colossal uniformity, this machine-like movement, this troubled spirit in pleasure itself, this exaggerated London, smothers the imagination and rends the heart . . . I anticipated great palaces, and saw nothing but mere small houses. But their very uniformity and their limitless extent impress the soul wonderfully.[5]

The setting produced by this combination of *laissez-faire*, economic development and their by-products – fifteen years of war to open the century followed by economic depression – represented the realization of the 'liberal city'. It stands as testimony to the distance between the theoretical ideal and reality.

The problems associated with understanding and confronting the transformations taking place inspired positions long considered philosophically and politically opposed: the proposals for alternative settlements described by the utopians of the period (Owen in 1817, Fourier in 1822) and partially realized in the years 1820–50, and the criticisms of Marx and Engels (1843, 1872)[6] regarding both spontaneous and planned industrial settlements. Both approaches rely on the assumption that city and territory could be transformed by means of a general transformation of society.

(4) The technical progress and entrepreneurial spirit which characterized this age did, none the less, make evident the need for infrastructural reorganization. In order to lay the railways, whether in straight or smoothly curving stretches, land rights were needed. While construction was carried out by private companies (except in Belgium), the task of acquiring the necessary land and

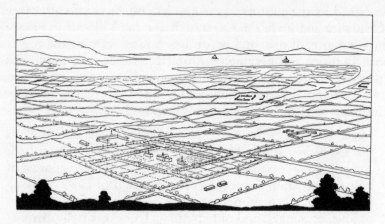

75 A 'village of harmony and co-operation': design attached to the report by Robert Owen, 1817.

devising a rational distribution of lines fell to the state. The Napoleonic law of 1810 regarding expropriation was further perfected under the July Monarchy in 1833 and again in 1841 on the eve of the national railway plan of 1842. This plan assigned monopolistic control of the principal lines to large firms, split the costs almost equally between public and private sources, and established that the railways would pass into state ownership after forty years. The process of 'forced acquisition' was legislated in England as well in 1842 and 1845, and the French law served as a model for that adopted in many other countries, including Italy in 1865.

Technical and juridical bases were established for the renewed confrontation between private initiative and public power. Expropriation was the exception which proved the rule of the general protection of private property; it was far less traumatic in the open countryside than in the cities, where individual interests made up a compact and complicated web. At the same time, the cholera epidemics which spread after 1830 produced a new philanthropic and reformist attitude in favour of public intervention to improve sanitary conditions in both old and new urban centres.

In England, Chadwick's 1842 report and the official inquiry of 1845 led to the first measures taken in London and then to the Public Health Act of 1848, which created a Board of Health.

Protests against these first urban interventions on the part of the public administration seem to us paradoxical. The radical *Economist* objected to the discussion of 'a great variety of matters which we cannot even enumerate, without crowding our space with a catalogue of somewhat offensive words' – like sewers, and rubbish – and warned that: 'suffering and evil are nature's admonitions; they cannot be got rid of; and the impatient attempts of benevolence to banish them from the world by legislation, before benevolence has learned their object and their end, have always been productive of more evil than good.'[7]

In France, this same reform became entangled with the revolution of 1848. The 1842 inquiry of the Societé de Saint-Vincent in Lille and the 1848 Blanqui report led to a proposed law, presented to the National Assembly by the de Melun brothers in 1849 and criticized by liberals and socialists alike. The law's presentation signalled clearly the significance of the innovation: 'The free use and free availability of that which belongs to the citizen requires the utmost respect', but 'nothing better justifies property than the authority of law which regulates its use.' The law of 1850 was more limited in scope than the English law of two years before, but includes in article 13 the following important provision: 'When insalubrity results from external and permanent causes and when these causes cannot be eliminated except by the undertaking of general works, then the commune can acquire, according to the procedure laid down in the law of 3 April 1841, all the land included within the area of these works.'[8]

In contrast to England, France had an efficient law for expropriation in addition to that for public health. This combination would prove to be an explosive one in the context of an authoritarian regime – that of Napoleon III – and an official determined to exercise his powers to their fullest extent – Baron Haussmann – and led to the spectacular trasnformation of Paris which would become the persuasive visual model for the transformation of European cities in the next half-century.

Haussmannization: The Post-Liberal City and its Problems

The above discussion of institutional developments was necessary in order to explain the decisive change which the 1860s represented

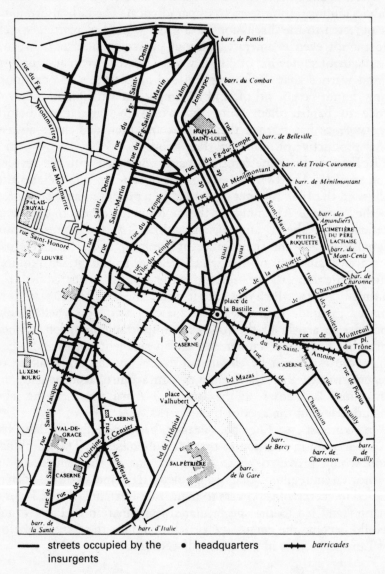

76 *Eastern Paris, showing the areas occupied by the insurgents in June 1848 (from M. Agulhon,* Nouvelle histoire de la France contemporaine, *VIII: 1848 ou l'apprentissage de la république,* Paris: Éditions du Seuil, *1973).*

for the European city. The city and its problems stood at the centre of human events in an entirely new way: no longer the symbol of power because of the historical link between the court and the capital, it became the mysterious and frightening source of power itself during a period of transition. The succession of French revolutions in 1789, 1794, 1799, 1830 and 1848 were all decided in Paris; and urban order became one of the central problems for the regimes that emerged from the battles of 1848 in various European countries: the French Second Empire, the constitutional empire of the Habsburg Franz Joseph, the new Tory governments of Disraeli in England and, a little later, the governments of the newly unified Germany and Italy.

It was the political emergency of defence against the revolutionary threat that led to renewed and decisive public intervention in the urban landscape. This intervention, however, ran into conflict with the established interests behind the victorious conservative regimes. A new compromise had to be found, one which went beyond the political circumstances of the moment and imposed a lasting change on the European city. In so far as it succeeded, this compromise sought to re-establish in the new technological and juridical context the traditional balance between public control and private initiative, between unity and multiplicity; it projected into the future that process described in the preceding chapters. In so far as it failed, it destroyed a part of the European tradition and paved the way for the dismantling of historic buildingscapes.

The crucial experiment took place in Paris and provided the rest of Europe with not only a functioning model, but also a concrete and compelling image. The example of Paris inspired individual and collective reactions which ran the gamut of emotions – marvel, excitement, sadness, regret, inurement – and overawed past images which faded in memory. This process was not the calculated effect of a political or cultural programme, but grew out of an adventurous confrontation of institutions and individuals; its resolution was more the product of chance than necessity.

The major role in this process was played by the career prefect Baron Haussmann who described his uncomplicated programme in 1850 on leaving the prefecture of Var: 'To bring together under the mantle of order and law, and for the just reconciliation of honest and disinterested opinion, all those men who are devoted without reserve to the good of the country and the great principles upon which society is based'.[9]

Seine prefect between 1853 and 1869, he conducted himself as an entrepreneur competing with many others who found space in the Bonaparte regime for their initiatives and in the process exhausted a range of theoretical orientations: Saint-Simonian, liberal, aristocratic. His assets included the personal support of the emperor, the legislative tools inherited from the July Monarchy and the Second Republic, and the efficiency of public technical and administrative offices. One at a time, he agreed and disagreed with everyone concerned as he expanded his intervention into all the various sectors of the urban mechanism. The limits of his field of play were defined by the successes and failures of his strategy, which eventually achieved a precarious but lasting balance between public control and private initiative in a large modern city.

One of the first tasks he faced was the creation of a service infrastructure for a city whose population had exceeded a million: sewers, water mains, gas lighting, public transportation, schools, hospitals, markets and parks. It had not yet been determined who should be in charge of these services, and private interests competed for control as well. The banker Laffitte proposed a private aqueduct fed by water raised from the Seine. Haussmann instead argued for public control and his view prevailed. The waterworks of the engineer Belgrand doubled the existing hydraulic network and tripled the amount of water supplied to the city. In this same period, the sewer system was almost completely rebuilt; the number of gas jets for public lighting tripled; bus services were integrated; a cab service was introduced; four large public parks were laid out; and the public structures necessary to the large city and eleven surrounding towns incorporated in 1859 were erected. These were the public works which would come to typify all European cities.

Modifications of the network of streets and surrounding urban fabric posed more complicated problems. Creation of wide and straight boulevards required the elimination of the unhealthy quarters and alleyways which had played an important role in the various revolts; a move intended to facilitate both sanitary measures and troop movements. On his side, Haussmann had article 13 of the 1850 public health law as well as a Senate decree of 1852 that authorized expropriation by executive order. He sought to main-

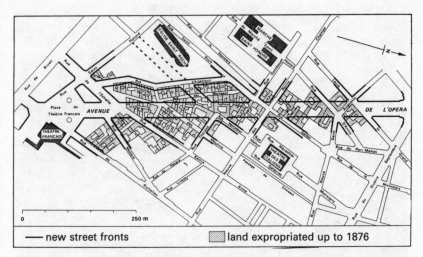

77   Paris: map of the demolitions for the construction of the Avenue de l'Opéra.

tain all of the expropriated land as public property and resell the building lots at their new commercial value. The State Council, however, frustrated his plans and in 1858 determined that the spaces around the new streets should be restored to the old owners.

Haussmann objected and in his memoirs wrote:

> The new decree gave property owners the right to keep lands not planned for public use after having paid the city for the structures and the cost of evicting the old tenants. In this way the expropriated property owner benefited from the increased value which his land had acquired thanks to the city, and the city lost the opportunity to recover to some degree the expenses incurred.[10]

However, he found himself alone in this position, facing not only the property owners and their political allies, but also the liberal left of Jules Ferry. Haussmann wrote in his memoirs: 'Even the emperor did not want to cross Monsieur Baroche [president of the state council] . . . moreover, his majesty showed little interest for problems of administrative procedure until they were translated into concrete, visible results.'[11]

78   Map of Paris in 1873 after Haussmann's reconstruction (from the

guide by A. Joanne, Paris: Hachette, 1873).

In this the emperor made a serious error. The 1858 decree had enormous visible consequences and changed for ever the shape of Paris and other European cities. It established a rigid boundary between public and private space, the building front, which replaced the complex reciprocal relationships characteristic of the earlier tradition. This situation created an economic imbalance between public administration and privately owned land. Property values inflated, which in turn created a public deficit and led to disfigurement of the urban environment. Overbuilding and high density raised property values while public services lagged behind, unable to keep up with the pace of private initiatives. The disparity created between property values within the city fed their upward spiral still more and worsened the environmental contrast between different sections of the urban organism.

This outcome depended upon the relative strength of the interests involved, but also upon the need somehow to define responsibility for urban activity and development, a responsibility that had become vague with time. The liberal phase of urban development came to a close with the need to agree upon a new model of city management, one which we might call 'post-liberal'. Haussmann won in his confrontation with Laffitte, but lost to Baroche. The armistice was settled along a line which became a recognizable boundary as conflict gave way to a precarious equilibrium, leaving an intense image that would endure in the collective memory.

We shall attempt to identify a few of the consequences which still apply today:

(1)   Public and private spaces, previously linked and interpenetrating to some degree, became distinct and in opposition. Protected by law and custom, private life is carried on in houses, apartments, workshops, offices and meeting halls; the importance of each of these environments correlates directly with its degree of isolation. We can imagine penetrating this veil of privacy only with the aid of a sorcerer who magically lifts off the urban rooftops for us. The sections of Parisian houses published in mid-century offer such a glimpse (illustration 79). Theatrical performances and collective celebrations also gained in distinction through exclusivity, and presentation in relatively small and closed spaces which bore no proportion to the size of the city. The theatre of Dionysus could accommodate almost the entire population of Athens; the

new Théâtre de l'Opéra in Paris has just over 2,000 seats for a city population of 2 million. Opposed to these private spaces are the public street and pavement, with their familiar and negative connotations, where we facelessly mix with everyone else and where Baudelaire felt alone among millions of others like himself.

The sphere of private sentiment and private interest, having only recently received legal guarantee, was a central collective concern and constant topic of theoretical treatises, literature and entertainment. One need only think of the novels and operas which systematically opposed private and public destiny: individuals accidentally present at important battles (Fabrizio del Dongo at Waterloo, Pierre Besuchov at Borodino); the love entanglements of Norma and Pollione and of Aida and Radames on which depended respectively the relationships between Gaul and Rome, between Egypt and Ethiopia. In the labyrinth of private spaces, all the aspirations and eccentricities of individuals and groups could be indulged, while the intervening public space of the street was lost and undistinguished. The system of land rents, by means of which public wealth was accumulated in private hands, accentuated the contrast between the two spheres. The passage from the private house to the public street entailed a qualitative decline in both detail and maintenance.

Haussmann's city was to assemble, for specific interests and purposes, a large number of independent spatial cells available for all sorts of activity and equipped with the best of modern technology. The branching system of streets, squares, and underground canals was a service structure which freed up these spaces and absorbed the contradictions of the system as a whole, beginning with economic contradictions, in order to keep them far from the spaces being served. A degree of decadence in these public structures was accepted as an accompaniment to well-being, to the wealth and beauty accumulated elsewhere behind the closed doors of private property.

Commercial exchange was the most suitable use for the building front that separated public from private, as it was an activity that took place astride the two spheres and so was able to make the most profitable use of this intermediate space. It was found that a triangular plan of streets, the one preferred by Haussmann and his followers, produced the greatest length of building front in a given area and the greatest number of the preferred corner positions. The

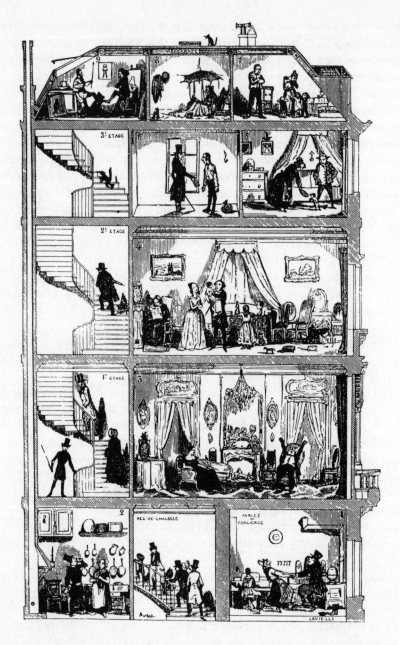

79   *Paris: vertical section of a five-storey house (from Hetzel,* Le Diable à Paris, *1845).*

favouring of commercial activity, however, disturbed other urban functions. For example, those living on the floors above were exposed both to the noise coming from below and to a degree of visual invasion. To avoid this inconvenience, it was necessary that a certain number of buildings be set back from the street and protected by a private space, a garden or courtyard. As a result, the block size shrank, the street front was no longer used and the building gained distinction.

Two characteristic models of the post-liberal city emerged out of this process: continuous building along the street front and independent structures isolated on private lots. The garden, once the province of palaces, had been reduced to a narrow strip of several metres surrounding the bourgeois private residence.

(2) The rigid separation of public and private space made for an ambiguous relationship with the old city out of which the new had evolved. The subtleties of the public–private relationship expressed by the system of streets, façades and buildings were pierced through. Building fronts conformed to the new dictates of profit, becoming alignments of interchangeable structures to be rebuilt at maturity according to the increasing value of their location. The nineteenth-century street derived from the medieval street, but ultimately modified and destroyed its predecessor. Ancient carriageways were enlarged; building fronts were rebuilt; excessively erratic layouts were eliminated and replaced by more regular designs.

In this way Hausmannization led to the destruction of historic city centres. A tendentious rhetoric came into being which exaggerated the decadence, insalubrity and squalor of the oldest parts of the city and became part of bureaucratic and celebratory language. In the Piazza della Repubblica, which replaced the medieval old market of Florence in 1890, an inscription reads: 'The old centre of the city, emerging from centuries of squalor, is given new life.' A typical aspect of this process was the opening of new, large streets cutting through a previously intricate web, revealingly described as operations of 'piercing' or 'gutting'. The knocking down of surrounding walls, an almost universal occurrence, represented a break with the ties of the past and the conquest of air, light and freedom of movement.

The most important of the old buildings were saved from destruction: those classified by art historians as historical documents and models (for the new building) of earlier styles, and those which in any case were held by the collective urban consciousness to be indispensable to each particular city's character. These structures were 'isolated' and used as perspective lenses focused on the new urban environment where, in any case, they lost their distinctiveness as the new denser style of building matched their dimensions. They stood as 'monuments' separate from the urban environment, just as the works of art in a museum are separated from one's daily sphere of activity.

There was in this situation the seed of the separation of art and life, the impoverishment of the daily environment and the transfer of beauty to the separate sphere of entertainment and free time. The world of culture noted this subconsciously; it would be the hidden cause of that uneasiness which we shall discuss below.

(3) Beginning in the 1850s, intellectuals generally distanced themselves from the mechanisms and results of public initiatives. Like Dickens, Eugène Sue, Balzac and Hugo all appreciated the confused, mysterious and integrated nature of the traditional city. The regularity, symmetry and technical complexity of Hauss-mann's city were criticized as vulgar and annoying novelties by authors as diverse as the Goncourts (in their *Journal* for 1860), Proudhon (in the description of a workers' meeting in 1863), Delvau (*Heures parisiennes*, 1866) and Sardou (*Maison Neuve*, 1866).[12] Positive evaluations came from an entirely different quarter. Blanc held that the sanitary improvements were necessary. Baron von Moltke and the deputy Picard praised almost contem-poraneously, in 1856, the advantages of the new straight streets for the maintenance of public order, since 'shot cannot take the first turn to the right'.[13]

Only Baudelaire refused to take part in this argument, uncon-vinced by either side. In his *Fleurs du mal*, dedicated to Hugo and already cited in the introduction to the present work, he captures the frightening rapidity of Haussmann's transformation, made possible by the establishment of the relationship between public and private intervention: the city was changing more quickly than a man's heart and no longer provided reassuring protection for the flow of human experience. Only human recollection could give meaning to a physical setting that had become precarious and temporary in the course of a single lifetime.

The overall result was in any case a loss of confidence on the part of intellectuals in the modern city. Maxime du Camp recalled in his *Souvenirs littéraires* that in about the year 1865 he went to the oculist for a new pair of glasses and, waiting for the lenses to be prepared, he began to watch the spectacle of the city from the Pont Neuf:

A raft covered with wood was floating down the Seine, and a bathing-station was being fixed to its moorings in the river. On shore I watched the smoke rising towards the clouds from the chimneys of the Hôtel des Monnaies, a cab rank along the Quai, and the omnibuses passing backwards and forwards, then a number of police-constables came out of the Prefecture, formed themselves into groups, and took their several ways; a prison-van appeared upon the Place Dauphine, and threaded its course among carriages and foot passengers; and a costermonger's cart was being pushed along near me. I know not why a scene I had so often witnessed should have struck me more than usual on that day.

Why did I suddenly seem to see evidence in the midst of the apparent confusion of organization and forethought? I cannot say, but at that moment I thought of Paris as of a great living organism having many members, set in motion by functions which acted with perfect regularity and accuracy. I fell into a reverie which was so much the more profound because of the noise and confusion round me. I remained rooted to the spot and absorbed in my new train of thought. When it began to grow dark I awoke from my dream, and then only did it occur to me that the optician had expected me two hours before. I had decided to study one by one and each in its turn the different springs which give impetus and movement to the complicated machinery of Paris life.[14]

In the years that followed he devoted enormous efforts to his six-volume work, *Paris, ses organes, ses fonctions et sa vie dans la seconde moitié du dix-neuvième siècle*, which appeared in 1869. Flaubert criticized his attempt 'to take Paris apart in order to describe its workings', instead of writing a novel that would be more realistic than any description, and said it was a mistake for du Camp 'to switch from a quill pen to a metal nib'. The huge mechanism du Camp sought to describe was, in any case, beyond his powers, and he succeeds only in communicating a sort of wondering awe.

The figurative arts also tried to establish contact with the new urban reality by way of the usual channels. Gustave Doré published books of etchings of Paris in 1861 and of London in 1872. The old and new cities are blended together in a picturesque image, and reality, placed upon a stage and obliquely illuminated, is subtly falsified. In this depiction, the artist exercised his freedom of expression ('artistic licence is the freedom to choose') and chose to represent a compelling spectacle, exaggerating the sources of distance and alienation. No judgement issued forth from this exploration, much less any suggestions on how to influence the transformation taking place. Dynamic reality was frozen in place and taken out of the flow of time in order to be reproduced and circulated.

Like Paris, London was a city in which projects for the rational control of public administration were the order of the day: the Thames embankments of 1848–65, the Metropolitan Railway of 1863, the clearance of unhealthy quarters of the city following the 1866 law on low-rent housing. The author of the text of the London volume, Blanchard Jerrold, described the world's largest city in tones like those used for Loti's voyages to the Orient or Whymper's climbing of the Alps. It was in fact the first attempt to capture in illustrated journalistic reportage that urban reality described in the social inquiries of a generation before; and while associated with the beginnings of the organized transformation of this reality, it succeeded neither in capturing nor in evaluating the process.[15]

Rather than limit the success of projects under way, these imperfect representations in some ways aided them, giving an impression of inevitability, the characteristic of so many other manifestations of 'progress'. The setting that was already emerging from the Parisian *grands travaux* in the 1860s pointed to concrete results and goals; this image of 'modernity' would captivate the civilized world for the next three-quarters of a century.

(4)   The models available to Haussmann, those used to give shape to the new Paris, were those provided by the artistic culture of his day. Ideological battles between the various movements for the revival of historical styles – Neoclassical, Neogothic etc. – did not lead to a preference for any one of these, but rather to their

coexistence in an expanded repertory, one that embraced models taken from all phases of European history and from exotic sources as well.

In the design of a particular building the choice between these various styles was an open one, but one that fitted poorly into the existing arrangement of urban spaces which were dominated by the large-scale perspective tradition of the seventeenth and eighteenth centuries (discussed in the previous chapter). The new ruling class, typified by Napoleon III and Haussmann, looked to this tradition, long associated with the centres of power, for the legitimation of their recent fortune, and, moreover, clearly preferred these forms, simplified and made banal by centuries of conventional repetition.

In spite of the attempt to maintain continuity between the creations of absolutist regimes and those of the ruling bourgeoisie, there was none the less a significant change of tone. The tension inherent in the projects of the Sun King derived from the contrast between ambitious, confident planning and inadequate execution, the result of precarious finance and administration. This tension had since been attenuated by a reverse combination: operative mechanisms that were finally effective together with mediocre planning, often reduced to a conventional stylistic veneer. Haussmann had much in common with Colbert – energy, meticulousness, patience, a sense of decorum – but Hittorf, Baltard and Garnier bore little resemblance to Le Brun, Le Nôtre and Hardouin-Mansart, and played a subordinate role relative to the more important administrators – like Alphand and Deschamps – who were the true leaders in Haussmann's projects.

Failures of design reveal themselves in the impaired ability to evaluate distance and spatial relations. Haussmann boasted that he always took the end-points of his boulevards into consideration, whether these consisted of existing monuments or new public buildings, like the railway stations or the Opéra. His terminal markers, however, were often too small in relation to the length of the streets or the width of the perspective corridors. Uselessly uniform surrounding structures virtually disappear in relation to the enormous dimensions of the principal streets and squares, the Étoile for example. Traffic and street furniture dominate, pushing architectural elements into the background; and the undulating contours of the terrain, not integrated in the plan, break the regularity of the two-dimensional design.

These characteristics escaped official culture and were masked in academic representations. They did appear, however, in the works of realist authors – Flaubert and Zola – and avant-garde artists who rejected the role demanded of the figurative arts – that of providing a respectable and amusing image of the new city. Instead they painted the pure form and colour of what they saw. The first collective show of the Impressionist painters was held in 1874 in the studio of the photographer Nadar – not a casual coincidence. In Monet's *Boulevard des Capucines*, painted in 1873, the architectural forms lose all recognizable stylistic form and become distant walls lined in dark and light. The 'rushing stream of faces of living men', described by Heine in 1828, became an army of similar shadows that no longer revealed 'the rainbow of their passions'. In what Corbusier would call the *rue corridor*, human individuals became things among things, while the inanimate things, poorly suited to human needs, revealed their precarious nature.

These painted images revealed the contrasts inherent in the new emerging urban setting and at the same time suggested the

80 Paris: Boulevard des Capucines *by Monet, 1873 (photo: Durand-Ruel, no. 5464).*

possibility of a new, open, changeable and unlimited setting which no one yet knew how to control; this quest would become the theme of future architectural research.

The method of urban planning described above and labelled 'Haussmannization' by contemporaries had a congenital defect: public expense was financed by private income, creating an open financial cycle. In seventeen years Haussmann spent about $2\frac{1}{2}$ thousand million francs; he received only 100 million from the state and did not increase taxes. Money was raised by borrowing, to be covered in the long term as public works contributed to urban growth – population increased from 1.2 to almost 2 million, and reached 3 million by the end of the century – and the increase of average income from 2,500 to 5,000 francs. As a result, tax revenues for the city of Paris grew from 20 to 200 million francs per year.

The cycle then could be completed, but only during the ascendant phase. Afterwards urban planning was dependent on the fluctuations of prices. When prices rose, planning went ahead; when they declined, it came to a halt. Following this rule, in the twenty years of inflation between 1850 and 1870 a large number of urban transformations were planned and executed throughout Europe: the works of Prefect Vaisse in Lyon; those of Mayor Anspach in Brussels; Poggi's plan for Florence, capital of the newly unified Italian state; the construction of the Ring in Vienna following the competition of 1857; the great public works of Bazalgette and the first underground railway system in London; Cerdá's plan for the enlargement of Barcelona; that of the prefect of police for Berlin; and Lindhagen's plan for Stockholm. Outside Europe one should also include the works undertaken in Mexico City during the brief empire of the Habsburg Maximilian, and the 'European' cities which sprang up next to indigenous cities throughout the colonial world.

The examples listed above confirmed the Parisian experiment in a large number of different contexts. The borrowing of formal models from previous historical periods, combined with the highlighting of earlier monuments as foci of the new urban structure, led to great variety in the new settings. On the one hand, it was the last attempt to maintain a degree of continuity with the history of the European city, to allow it to grow and adapt to new technical demands while keeping to an earlier template by the conscious employment of forms inherited from the past. On the other hand, historical urban and structural forms were used schematically as models for modern planning, and this led to the destruction of a large part of the earlier setting: the widening of streets, the isolation of 'monuments' and the substitution of stylistic copies for earlier structures. Europe began to squander its historical patrimony, preserving certain elements in museums or in the new open urban spaces, which functioned as outdoor museums. The best results were obtained in those cases where the overall design assigned distinct spaces to the new and the old: Barcelona, where the old city sits isolated and undisturbed in its *ensanche*; or Vienna, where the ring of modern structures was inserted between medieval centre and Baroque periphery. Attempts at montage instead led sooner or later to the complete destruction of the pre-modern organism (Milan, Brussels).

During the subsequent two decades of declining prices, from 1870 to 1890, all of these projects suffered a general slowing down, and conditions hampered the initiation of new ones. In Paris, the debit left by Haussmann would be balanced only at the century's end. By chance it was in just this period that a call was raised for the transformation of Rome, which was annexed to the kingdom of Italy in 1870. It quickly became apparent that this project exceeded the means of the public administration, and the attendant delay was not subsequently made up.

From 1890 another favourable period began, and urban development was relaunched in an organized fashion. Large unfinished public works programmes were completed: the underground railways of Berlin (1896), Paris (1900) and Vienna (1904); and above all the great programmes of low-rent housing undertaken to close the gap between supply and demand created by the growth of speculation. These programmes stemmed in England from the 1885 Housing of the Working Classes Act, in Germany from the Adickes law of 1901, in France from the Société Française des Habitations à Bon Marché of 1890, and in Italy from the Istituti per le Case Popolari of 1902. In this same period, the garden city movement began in England, spreading to the rest of Europe in the first two decades of the twentieth century, and urban planning became a recognized discipline based on the treatises of Baumeister (1876), Stübben (1890) and Unwin (1909).[16]

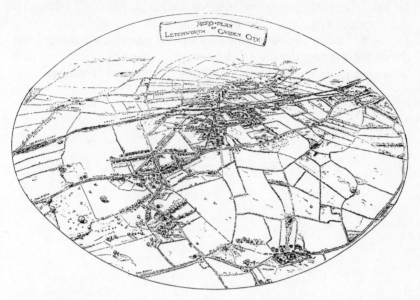

81 Bird's-eye view of Letchworth Garden City (from C. R. Ashbee, Where the Great City Stands, London: Essex House Press, 1917).

Land rents, an integral part of the method of urban transformation, facilitated the process in the short run, but represented a serious mortgage and impaired both the rationality and the refinement of the results: generally too dense and with too few public spaces, the building and urban typologies employed were compromised from the outset. The settlement of accounts between public administration and landowning interests established an inappropriate setting for the most important decisions, excluding not only the eventual users, but also the specialists – technicians and artists – necessary to the construction of the new cities. Those in the latter categories who refused to accept a marginal role were forced to work in a new condition of isolation.

So began, in the second half of the nineteenth century, the long itinerary of avant-garde culture which attempted to circumvent dominant interests and discover the possible ways to a new productive and organizational structure and to a new urban environment. The starting-points were many: the solitary dreams of Baudelaire, the severe writing of Flaubert, Morris's reform of the applied arts, and the impassive craft of the Impressionist painters. Architects were slow to join this movement, and did not do so till the last decade of the century, when the confrontation became a more even one and the 'new' a practical hypothesis.

Europe in the Contemporary World

Cities of the Europeanized World

The events which revolutionized Europe and its cities in the nineteenth century also served to establish European dominance throughout the globe. In the sixteenth century the technical and organizational skills of the European states had enabled them to sail their ships to all the continents of the world, but only in the sparsely populated New World did they manage complete penetration. Elsewhere they came up against existing and equally powerful states. Later, in the nineteenth century their superiority was so great as to allow the occupation and subjugation of all other countries. In 1884, when the Congress of Berlin negotiated the partitioning of Africa, this process was almost complete.

The huge number of settlements either built or transformed during the period of European colonization certainly merit independent treatment; no such work exists and an attempt of the sort would exceed the scope of the present volume. The importance of this process for our purposes is the way in which it reveals the character and limitations of the European urban tradition. In various parts of the world, Europeans encountered one another, in addition to the indigenous peoples, and so acquired a self-consciousness different from what it had been before.

Most of the new overseas European settlements of the second half of the nineteenth century and the twentieth century fit the post-liberal model. However, even those from the early nineteenth century foreshadow in a surprising way later methods and models. In Europe, the compromises of Haussmannization developed out

of the competition between public intervention and private interests in high-density areas. Outside Europe, the availability of
large open spaces and the role of public initiative, present and
decisive from the outset, led early on to the same results. One
could say that outside Europe the liberal phase was skipped over,
allowing a direct transition from the pre-industrial to the post-
liberal.

The English took the lead, founding the largest number of these
settlements. In India, the coastal bases of the seventeenth century
gradually grew to become the principal cities, while several new
towns were founded as summer retreats for the Europeans: Simla
in 1827 and Darjeeling in 1835. The military and commercial base
of Singapore was strategically established at the mouth of the Strait
of Malacca in 1819. The urbanization of Australia began after the
juridical reforms of the 1820s: to the penal colony of Sydney,
founded in 1788, were added Melbourne (1835), Adelaide (1836)
and Brisbane (1840). The French occupied Algeria in 1830 and
enlarged the existing coastal cities. During the Second Empire they
colonized Indochina and in 1865 began the enlargement of Saigon,
eliminating completely the original village. The fate of Greece,
liberated from the Turks in 1829, was similar. The German-born
King Otto designated Athens as the new capital, and the city was
rebuilt in 1834 according to the plan of Leo von Klenze. Other
cities carrying the same mythical names as the nearby ancient sites
were also founded: Sparta (1834), Corinth (1858) and Thebes
(1861). Along the Suez canal three new cities were built – Port Said
in 1859, Port Tewfik and Ismailia in 1862 – in the same period that
witnessed the initiation of the modernization project for Cairo.
The Russians began the urbanization of their vast Asian possessions and in 1860 founded Vladivostock, end-point of the Trans-
Siberian railway on the Pacific Ocean.

In all of these cases a new regular design was implemented
without difficulty. The pre-existing settlements – including the
Turkish villages occupying the famous sites of ancient
Greece – were pushed to the side and not combined with the new
to create a single organism. The principle of separateness for
Europeans and natives encouraged this practice and easily overcame historical and artistic curiosity regarding local traditions.
Native settlements were either destroyed (Saigon) or else occupied
an inferior position next to the European city (Athens, Algiers,

Tunis); in the former case, the colonial city required construction of new indigenous quarters either permanent or temporary.

The particular and non-universal character of the development model defined after the mid-nineteenth century emerges from this process. The post-liberal model was well suited to the compact settlements of Europe, while in sparser settlements, especially in the United States, the urban planning introduced by the first colonists – the gradual and discontinuous occupation of a vast territory according to a pre-established geometric grid – could continue indefinitely. This simpler American model would subsequently spread on an international scale. Only at a more advanced stage of development, when modification of the existing urban fabric became an issue, were imitations of European models grafted on, often for decorative reasons. The 'city beautiful' movement born in America in the late nineteenth century was an example of the latter process.

The eclectic culture of Europe, employed to shape the surfaces where public and private spaces intersected, could theoretically incorporate traditions from throughout the world. Exotically styled buildings were displayed at the Paris International Expositions beginning in 1867 and catalogued in Viollet-le-Duc's *Histoire de l'habitation humaine* of 1875. However, these historical traditions were made part of the European cultural world only after having been reduced to 'styles', a process which required their first being interpreted through the medium of perspective which distinguished between formal and structural elements. And it was only at the level of individual structures that these traditions were adopted; as already observed, the seventeenth- and eighteenth-century tradition of composition remained dominant on the general scale of urban design, and it was this latter tradition which gave the new urban settings their compactness. All of these factors contributed to prevent recognition of the original characteristics of non-European urban settlements and their incorporation in the new colonial cities. Even the terminology employed – building scale and urban scale, monuments and common buildings, roads, squares, building lots etc. – derived from the peculiarities of the European experience, which clearly emerged in the confrontation with settings produced by different historical experiences.

Another instance of the difficulty inherent in a true confrontation was created by the 'modernization' of distant countries. In

China, the 1842 Treaty of Nanking opened five ports to foreigners. One of these was Shanghai, still a small fortified city but preferred by foreign agents because it offered the possibility of avoiding confrontation with a large traditional settlement, and also a strategic position at the mouth of the principal navigable river, the Yangtze. Lacking any general urban plan – after 1860 the European settlements became 'extraterritorial concessions' with their own laws – Shanghai grew rapidly and became by the century's end the largest city in China.

In Japan, the new ruling class which seized power after the ending of isolationism in 1853 quickly overcame subjugation to foreign powers and began that country's spectacular modernization. In 1868 the imperial capital was transferred from Kyoto to Edo, renamed Tokyo, capital of the East. Edo had been the Shogun capital; from 1633 all the local vassals together with their families were required to live there, and the 1785 population numbered 1.4 million. A series of events radically altered the city's general functioning: the law of 1872, which introduced private ownership of land; the administrative reform of 1878, which created a system of fifteen districts (*ku*); and the establishment of public services, including the telegraph (1869), postal service (1871), railways (1872) and gas lighting (1874). The population had fallen to 600,000 in 1872, and then grew again to 1.37 million in 1889 and 3.36 million by the first census of 1920.

Whether regulated by a general plan or not, these transformations led to a much more definitive break with the past than did those in Europe. The cities of the Asian world were traditionally subject to a higher authority which administered an enormous area and controlled hierarchically the relationships between social groups and individuals. This power, translated into European terms, became the state which now confronted private citizens made equal by recent legal guarantees; between the two was an intermediate space not filled by an autonomous and authoritative local administration able to create specific systems of norms for each city. This route to 'modernization' consisted of the introduction of a property law based on liberal European and American institutions; it suddenly authorized the free use of property by private interests according to a collection of weak and generic public regulations which did not adequately represent the general interests of citizens. In Japan, institutional reforms were introduced with the 1889 constitution, based on the contemporary French and German models. The result with regard to the management of urban areas was a strictly liberal regime, not subsequently corrected and in fact reaffirmed in the 1947 constitution imposed by the victorious Americans. This regime has stood in ever greater contrast with the country's economic development, so that today a superdeveloped Japan carries with it the burden of uncontrolled land speculation which wreaks havoc with the cities and, from time to time, with the stock market as well. If Japan had modernized a generation later, it would have adopted instead the more advanced urban planning practices and legislation of the later English and German models, and would be today a different country.

These examples highlight the specificity and impossibility of translation of European urban institutions at the decisive phase of world colonization. Haussmann's model, based on the division of urban space between administration and private real estate, represented the schematic translation of a recurring theme in European history: the balance between collective control and individual initiative. It could only function when both of these were adequately represented. Its standard features were reproduced by nostalgic colonizers throughout the globe, exciting admiration as evidence of European superiority, and while they suited European cities to a degree, they conflicted hopelessly with those overseas.

The *rue-corridor* derived from the medieval and Baroque public street, on to which opened the façades of the bordering houses was entirely incompatible with both the Islamic/eastern streets, which linked together houses facing on to interior courtyards, and with the ceremonial avenues of the Asian capitals, which were instead axial successions of enclosures. The arrival of the automobile – which could not pass through the Islamic streets, broke open the ceremonial avenues and could not be freely manoeuvred even in the Haussmannian public spaces – opened up the conflict. And in fact, over the past seventy years asphalt streets have almost entirely destroyed the traditional settings of non-European cities.

In conclusion, the technical and legal mechanisms imported from Europe created the same crisis situations in other continents during the twentieth century that they had in Europe in the first half of the nineteenth: crowding, disorder, public health problems, unbridled speculation and a lack of public regulations. A new, habitable setting has not yet emerged out of these upheavals. The disastrous conflict between human life and the constructed environment still needs identification and correction. The task of documentation has only just begun: Turner, Abrams and Payne have published the first analyses,[1] comparable to those of Chadwick, Blanqui and Villermé on European cities 150 years before. The subsequent task of proposals and experimentation has been confronted sporadically in India, Brazil and Egypt in the face of enormous and so far prohibitive political, economic and cultural obstacles.

The Invention of a New City

The cultural debate taking place during the second half of the nineteenth century and the first decades of the twentieth was fully played out in the international confrontation described above: confrontation with past traditions, the balance between public and private spheres, and the definitive continuation in an industrialized world of the city's Aristotelian role as a tool for realizing the perfection of human existence.

As already mentioned, intellectuals found the sudden changes resulting from the experiments in 1850s Paris and the rest of Europe disconcerting, and the prevailing reaction was one of detachment and rejection. None the less, out of this reaction a new itinerary developed which led over the next half century to the rethinking and revision of the cultural and organizational bases of the city.

Flaubert deliberately severed connections with the practical nature of the events taking place and contributed to neither their understanding nor revision. However, by affirming the superiority of the novel over conventional accounts he asserted that the human condition took precedence over all exterior generalizations. In 1871, passing in front of the ruins of the Tuileries, destroyed by the *Communards*, he remarked enigmatically: 'If *L' Éducation sentimentale* had been understood, none of this would have happened.' In the third part of that novel, written between 1867 and 1869, he temporarily abandoned the narrator's restrained role and openly compared the mediocre but authentic adventure of Frédéric with Rosannette to the senseless events of June 1848. Indeed mediocrity – and later idiocy in *Bouvard et Pécuchet* – would be the end-point of his literary experience, which came to a close amid a suffocating accumulation of '*idées reçues*'.

Baudelaire sought to escape from the spleen of the modern city either to the past, by means of individual memory, or towards the future, by means of the still more fragile mechanism of dreams. Estrangement was so great in his 1861 *Rêve parisien* that it seemed to capture among the usual exotic and Delacroix-like images a scrap of the future:

> Le sommeil est plein de miracles!
> Par un caprice singulier,
> J'avais banni de ces spectacles
> Le végétal irrégulier,
>
> Et, peintre fier de mon génie
> Je savourais dans mon tableau
> L'enivrante monotonie
> Du métal, du marbre et de l'eau[2]

Also part of this large work, 'Le voyage', dedicated to Maxime du Camp, becomes a symbol – loaded with both subjective and objective significance – of the flight from the present to a destination neither described nor describable, but necessary just the same: 'Au fond de l'Inconnu pour trouver du *nouveau*!'.[3]

In the 1861 edition this last word was set in italics according to the instructions of the author. It soon became the motto of that part of the literary and artistic world that broke away from official culture (Manet in fact began his career at the 1861 Salon; the first Salon des Refusés was held in 1863). The following generation inspired the avant-garde movements for the renewal of architecture and applied arts – Art Nouveau, Jugendstil, Liberty – which after 1890 promoted a new style and a new emotionally loaded rapport between individual and individual, artist and public.

Certain *fin de siècle* artists (Horta, Van de Velde, Olbrich, Hoffmann, Voysey, Mackintosh) called for the immediate, and piecemeal, renewal of the urban and domestic setting, and to this end agreed to a hasty, and untimely, participation in its formal mechanisms. Regional schools flourished in Belgium, Holland, Scotland, Catalonia and Austria, and succeeded in renewing the European figurative repertory; in a few cases inroads were made regarding urban planning (Wagner in Vienna, Berlage in Amsterdam). Other artists, Cézanne and Matisse for example, refused to participate in urban projects and retreated into their studios, where they gradually dismantled the formal apparatus on which the management of cities had been based, constructing the basis for a more radical and long-term renewal.

Alongside research of the type described above, committed from the outset to the discovery of the new, other avenues developed which were more closely tied to the present and based on a scientific approach to urban problems. A series of partial, but accurate, and above all cumulative, criticisms arose out of the existing urban contradictions; at first these were aimed at the correction of individual distortions of the post-liberal city, but ultimately they led to the outlining of a different sort of planning and management altogether.

Pressure created by the development of income property caused housing costs to exceed levels that were affordable to the lower classes, who none the less remained an integral part of the city and its functioning. Cities became dense and congested, lacking space for public services. Larger industry and plants were forced out to the periphery and moved progressively farther out as the cities expanded. When urban planning came into being as a specialized discipline at the end of the nineteenth century, it brought proposals for reform aimed at the correction of these problems: programmes for low-rent housing subsidized with public funds; the 'garden city' immersed in greenery; and the 'industrial city' designed to accommodate industry as well as the other urban functions.

In the first two decades of the twentieth century the two approaches described above encountered one another:

1   The acceleration of artistic investigation led to the exhaustion of the entire repertory of forms accumulated in the past and the artist as a result came up against a 'naked wall',[4] opening the way to entirely new sorts of invention.

2   As the scale of subsidized and experimental public projects grew – whole quarters of public housing, the garden city – practical experimentation suggested that public urbanization might emerge as an alternative method for urban development and a key to the modern re-establishment of the balance between individual and collective choice. Public administration and developers split tasks between themselves in a chronological, as op-

posed to spatial, way. City governments acquired property to be transformed, put it in order and then gave over those parts designated for construction to private and public developers in a situation of economic parity. The design of an overall plan became possible, without the obstacle of property lines, and of individual buildings, without the pressures of income property. Urban space opened up to a new sort of planning in which there was again a place for artistic culture, itself finally freed of the constraints of the past.

The two lines converged towards a common result: on the one hand the reintroduction of artistic innovation at the various scales of urban planning, and on the other the transformation of planning into a rational combination of public and private interests, made compatible, within a framework of the rules of the market and entrepreneurial competition. The Neoplastic artists – Van Doesburg, Mondrian – were vividly aware that at stake was the possibility of relocating artistic investigation in everyday life. It is no coincidence that one of them, Cor Van Eesteren, became in 1928 the director of the first great experiment in modern planning: that for Amsterdam approved in 1934. Mondrian put it like this:

> Imperfect and characterized by dry necessity, the modern environment and life itself come up short. Art becomes a refuge where we seek the beauty and harmony that are lacking and vainly looked for in that life and environment. Beauty and harmony have become unattainable goals, located in the world of art but banished from life. (1922)

> In the future, the realization of pure plastic expression in palpable reality will replace the work of art. But in order to achieve this, orientation toward a universal conception and detachment from the oppression of nature is necessary. Then we will no longer have the need of pictures and sculpture, for we will live in realized art . . . 'Art' is only a 'substitute' as long as the beauty of life is deficient. It will disappear in proportion as life gains in equilibrium. (1942)[5]

'Modern architecture', as it would be called, succeeded in gathering together a number of different strands, each in search of resolution: the exhaustion of post-cubist investigation in painting, the search for a new integrated system of values following the tragedy of the First World War, the great programmes for post-war

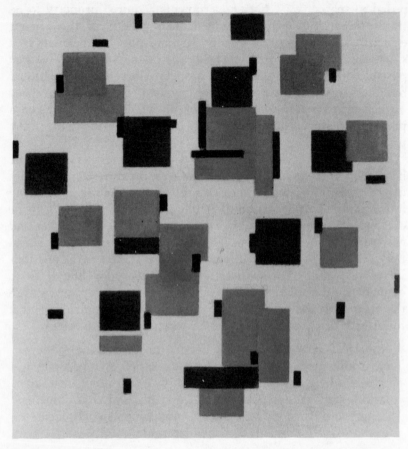

82   *P. Mondrian,* Composition in Blue, *1917 (Kroller-Mueller Museum, Otterlo, © DACS 1993).*

reconstruction, and the beginnings of the scientific understanding of individual and collective behaviour. It was an exceedingly brief episode – restricted to the period between the economic renewal of 1924 and the crisis of 1929 – but it engendered a lasting change in European culture. In Gropius's Bauhaus (1919–28) a diverse group of planners managed to collaborate, and out of this melting-pot there emerged the most original and remarkable architectural experiments that Europe had witnessed in many centuries, those of Mies van der Rohe, Le Corbusier and Aalto.

83a and b   Berlin: two views (façade and interior) of the Modern Art
Gallery by Mies van der Rohe (photos: Benevolo).

This episode represented the climax of European artistic culture; it succeeded both in severing ties with the specifically European tradition and in offering a conceptual basis for modernization throughout the world. In the section that follows we shall consider the consequences for Europe, but first we must look at its more general consequences which changed the way of perceiving, and changing, the city.

In order to break free from the limitations of post-liberal theory and practice, it was necessary to start again with a clean slate and shed the enormous accumulation of conventional forms received from the past. Together with Flaubert's *'idées reçues'*, the historical European tradition, now little more than a collection of styles, had become unusable. This unloading made possible the creative and experimental outburst of the 1920s, the product of artists born in the last two decades of the nineteenth century. It also allowed a new link with the inheritance of the past based on critical detachment, and so open and limitless with regard to the entire range of human experience. An objective understanding of the entire series of human interventions in the landscape was recouped by sacrificing the subjective continuity of European experience. The task in hand was the re-establishment of a responsible, gradual and collective approach to the ordering of the constructed setting, and so the avoidance of tendentious and artificial 'modernities'.

The role of the city as a partial setting, in opposition to the open countryside, became of necessity problematic. The new planning took as its canvas the entire geographic environment, and on this canvas the city would require redefinition.

Urban functions were identified – living, working, the care of the body and the spirit, and communication – and their character-istics defined in opposition to the post-liberal city. The most important element of the city became the home, where the greater part of the day was spent. It was, however, inseparable from the services which acted as its extensions. Production determined the three fundamental types of human settlement: cities spread throughout the countryside, the linear industrial cities and the radial centres of trade. Recreational activities required an abun-dance of free space, and this space could not be confined to specific areas; instead, one large space was needed in which all the other elements were freely distributed. The nineteenth-century park anticipated the new city, itself a huge park equipped for all the

requirements of urban life. Communication was organized according to the various means of transportation and the *rue-corridor* was
replaced with a system of separate paths for pedestrians, bicyclists,
slow and fast vehicles, all traced out in the continuous space of the
park-city.

City building took as its starting-point the basic elements of its
various functions, and built on these by the application of typical
and repeatable solutions. The basic functional element of the home
was not the building – whether private dwelling or block of
flats – but the actual living-space. Starting with this living-space,
traditional methods of composition were dissected and alternative
methods studied that would be more responsive to a range of old
and new requirements. The first attempts along these lines often
led to utopian or approximate results, but without this conscious
breaking away it would not have been possible to confront
seriously the problems of modern city planning, to identify the
many needs to be addressed, and to exploit the richness of local
traditions once divorced from a schematic catalogue of styles.

This methodology did not represent a final stylistic choice to be
imposed on building techniques, but instead aimed to unify these
techniques in order to deal in a rigorous way with problems of
both individual sectors and the composition as a whole. It was

84　*Design for modern city organization by Le Corbusier (from his* La
Ville radieuse, *Paris: Vincent, Fréal, 1964; 1st edn 1933).*

again Mondrian who stated that 'art and technique are inseparable', or rather must once again be brought together as they had been until two centuries before. Beginning at that moment when European science and technology became necessary points of reference for the entire world, a scientific approach to city planning served to distinguish the general contributions of the European urban model that were universally applicable from its more particular and specific aspects. It was an approach that would salvage and promote, in a modern sense, local traditions from around the world.

The Renewal of the European City in the Past Fifty Years

The cultural change described above, whose universal and systematic value we clearly recognize today, grew out of concrete and profoundly disturbing events. The change occurred in Europe after the First World War, and it was the shock of this experience that enabled European culture to achieve a degree of detachment from itself and critically evaluate its past. The period of material and moral reconstruction during the following decade provided the appropriate setting. After 1929 economic crisis and eventually the Second World War led to the cancellation of most long-term planning and engendered instead projects responding to a climate of emergency. After the Second World War, the division of Europe into separate blocks cut the continent in half and imposed limits – in the east, but also to a degree in the west – on both discussion and experimentation. The changes of 1989, whatever their consequences may be, removed this division and have opened the way for a unified approach to the problems and opportunities of the European experience at the end of the twentieth century.

Urban planning depends upon numerous factors – cultural, institutional, economic – which can be co-ordinated only with great difficulty. As a result, the new ideas which came to fruition in the inter-war period led to many model individual structures, a few building complexes and quarters, and only one important urban planning project in a major city. The first category, well illustrated in books on the history of architecture, includes (to cite only the most important buildings of 1929): the Villa Savoye in Poissy, the Tugendhat house in Brno, the Columbushaus in Berlin, the Paimio sanatorium, the Van Nelle factory in Amsterdam, and the

Narkomfin house in Moscow. Medium-size public projects were undertaken by Oud in Rotterdam and in Weimar Germany by May (Frankfurt) and Martin Wagner (Berlin). The only large-scale planning venture was that for Amsterdam laid out between 1928 and 1934 under the direction of Van Eesteren and fully carried out over the next thirty years, in spite of interruption during the German occupation of 1940–5. Van Eesteren's plan employed the centuries-old practice of preventive land reclamation which had previously made possible the plan of 1609 and its completion over the course of the seventeenth century.

In Amsterdam for the first time the basic difference between the new periphery – a free montage of basic functional elements – and

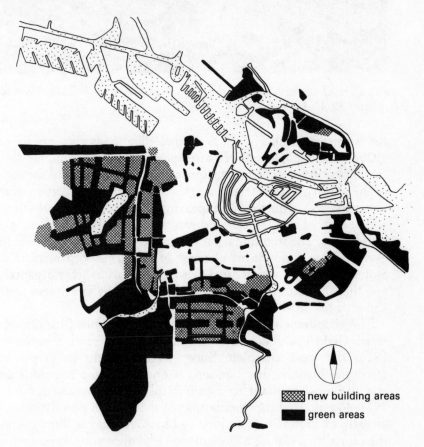

new building areas

green areas

85   *Planning design for Amsterdam, 1934.*

86   *Part of the western outskirts of Amsterdam with Lake Sloterplas (photo: KLM Aerocarto).*

the semicircular Baroque city – including additions up to the 1920s – was recognized. No attempt was made to combine these two by means of the Haussmannization of the latter, and the order of the old city was preserved in its original form. Unification of the two parts was achieved by employing the external natural setting, which entered into the city and served to separate the old and new settlements. The traditional park acquired a new structural role and even became a dominant element of the urban organism: Lake Sloterplas around which the new western quarters were organized; and the 900-hectare wood created from new in a sandy area to the south of the city.

The encounter in Britain between the domestic (Ruskin, Howard, Geddes) and continental traditions set in motion in the late 1930s the most complete European experiment in urban and territorial planning for London, at once the most populous city and the most resistant to a general plan. The Barlow report of 1937–40 criticized the distribution of the English population, and as early as 1938 it was decided to block the further expansion of the capital by creating a circumference of open countryside which persists to this day, the 'green belt'. During the war the London

87 United Kingdom development plan (London Central Office of Information, 1968).

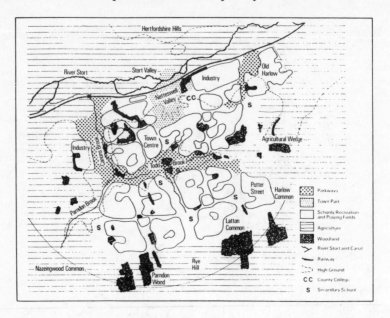

88   Outline plan for Harlow New Town (from F. Gibberd, B. Hyde Harvey and L. White, Harlow: The Story of a New Town, *Harlow Development Corporation, 1980).*

plan came under discussion, and in 1944 Abercrombie and Forshaw's project was approved; this called for a reorganization of the area within the green belt, with an eye to lowering population density, and the development of several new publicly supported cities outside this circumference. In 1946 the national 'new towns' project was launched, eight to be established around London and six in other parts of the country. The first practical results led to renewed debate and modifications. Additional new towns were founded in the 1950s and 1960s; though they were initially planned to accommodate about 50,000 inhabitants each, this figure was increased to 100,000 and in one case (Milton Keynes) to 250,000. Development corporations were created by the national government to draw up urban plans, and prepare and resell the land. In this way several million people were settled without expenditure of public funds; it seems in fact, according to Osborn and Whittick's book, originally published in 1963, that a small profit was rea-

89   London: the Roehampton Estate (photo: Benevolo).

lized.[6] The best resources of English architecture were employed in an effort to reconcile the traditional desire to live amidst greenery with the creation of an urban environment; the new settings achieved both privacy and habitability.

Neutral during the war, Sweden executed careful plans for the expansion of Stockholm and other cities in the 1940s and 1950s, paying particular attention to variety in the buildingscape and insertion into the surrounding terrain. Swedish models were both admired and imitated by other European countries that set about the work of post-war reconstruction.

Reconstruction in France began in a regressive institutional and cultural setting. The commissions awarded to Le Corbusier in Marseille and to Perret in Le Havre and Amiens stand out as irrelevant exceptions. It was only under the Fifth Republic that the decision was made to undertake large-scale public urbanization. The *zones à urbaniser en priorité* (ZUP) introduced in 1958 were

90   Aerial view of Cumbernauld New Town (photo: Aerofilms Ltd, no. A 167154).

important for their size – as large as 100,000 inhabitants – but conventional as regards typology and environmental results. The later *villes nouvelles* planned between 1965 and 1970 were instead linked to a national plan to counter the conglomeration of population in Paris and provide a degree of balance by means of the *métropoles d'équilibre* (Lille–Roubaix-Turcoing, Nancy–Metz, Strasbourg, Lyon–Saint-Étienne, Marseille, Toulouse, Bordeaux and Nantes). Five *villes nouvelles* were planned around Paris, and four more near Lille, Rouen, Lyon and Marseille. Although the new settlements were large, designed to accommodate 300,000–400,000 inhabitants, they were none the less conceived with an eye to both formal and environmental problems. Demand, however, was overestimated, and growth projections of the 1960s – 14 million inhabitants in the Paris area and 75 million in France by the year 2000 – were revised in the following decade, and the perceived central problem of growth was gradually replaced by that of redistribution.

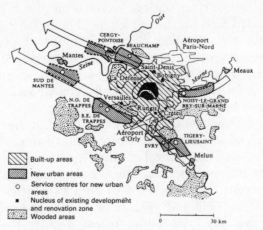

91   Outline plan for the Paris region, Schéma Directeur, 1969 (source: M. P. Merlin).

Germany faced the task of rebuilding an urban heritage largely destroyed in the Second World War. Reconstruction began in the context of an evolved but unrenewed legal framework and without ambitious plans. The lasting results of this phase are the centres of many large and medium-sized cities in which the careful restoration of the destroyed monuments did not extend to the general urban fabric, often trivialized by a general neglect of the buildingscape. Only after 1960 did the large-scale projects of the various *Länder* (or other geographical subdivisions) surface; among these the Ruhr plan of 1966 stands out. Economic development quickly ended this first phase and triggered the subsequent development of individual architectural projects for the more important cities: Frankfurt, Hamburg, Munich. The dense network of existing cities obviated the need for new cities: the existing urban centres were all of manageable size – Berlin remained distinct and isolated – and the careful expansion of a few secondary cities – Wolfsburg, Duisburg – was sufficient. In 1984 a large programme of urban renewal was attempted in Berlin, based on the nineteenth- and twentieth-century pattern of streets; since 1989 and the breaking down of the Wall, however, the greater and more pressing problem of the combination of the two cities has taken precedence, a project which will require courageous and large-scale modifications.

In Holland, high-level urban planning continued as programmes for environmental control on a national scale gained momentum:

regulation of the river outlets, reclamation of the Zuiderzee, and the integrated plan for the semicircle of cities from Amsterdam to Rotterdam, the so-called *Randstad*, aimed at preventing their melding together by preserving the undeveloped intermediate spaces. Though not spurred by such serious problems, the Scandinavian countries, Switzerland and Austria all achieved an acceptable balance between city and country.

Italy and Spain, on the other hand, failed in the transition to a plan which encompassed the entire national territory. The dictatorships blocked the renewal of urban legislation that characterized the rest of Europe, and this situation was only confirmed by the vested interests that continued to hold sway after the return of democracy, in 1945 and 1975 respectively. The huge amount of building that has gone on in recent decades has been almost entirely the product of private development. Enormous suburbs, the malformed results of speculation, have grown up around the old city centres, while municipal planning is guided by no general programme. This situation has led to the occasional interesting structure, but not to the creation of satisfactory urban environments. In recent years, after most of the damage had been done, attempts have been made to remedy the disastrous settings in some cities, ingenious efforts that in a few cases have met with success: the programme for the renewal of Barcelona and of several medium-size Italian cities (Bologna, Modena, Brescia).

In eastern Europe, nationalization of property has not improved the urban setting, but instead has destroyed the fundamental character of the cities, eliminating the dialectic between general and particular decisions. Unlimited public discretion with regard to the organization and use of urban space in the absence of confrontation with private initiatives opened the door to arbitrary choices, lacking in motivation or significance. The great collective projects, responding to architectural whim and not required to meet the needs of communication and commerce, have not stood up to the test of time, suffering rapid deterioration.

The attempt to rationalize public planning, especially evident in Poland, failed to avoid the amplification of errors along the way, nor could it compensate for the ageing of technical tools. Now that these experiments have been stripped of their political cover, a disastrous picture is revealed: ecological destruction, huge suburbs of multi-storey apartment buildings which are literally falling to pieces and appear to be irreparable, unfinished public spaces and the destruction of privacy in cities both large and small. In Czechoslovakia, spared from wartime destruction, the survival, whether intentional or by chance, of a few perfectly preserved old cities (Cesky Krumlov, Hradec Kralove, Kutna Hora) is striking, though bought at an unacceptable price in terms of economic and social limitations; clearly this situation cannot endure long into the future.

This varied picture, with both its merits and its defects, seems today to be on the road to general stabilization, a situation much different from that of the rest of the world still undergoing dramatic growth and change. Population in Europe is no longer increasing; new building takes place at a modest rate; and industrial plants are modernized without expansion or are even dismantled. While internal transformation may be difficult, especially in the east, it is none the less a finite task. Future economic, social and political changes will alter the physical setting less dramatically and will make only more evident the need for a balanced environment in which the qualitative improvement previously prevented by the scale and rapidity of change may be realized.

From this point of view, the historical richness of the urban settings acquires renewed importance. What remains of the pre-industrial city assumes greater value than what has been added subsequently. Although only a small part of the buildingscape, it none the less dominates the overall framework and provides both the city's identity and a point of reference for the collective imagination – not to mention the presence there of artistic and cultural wealth, the monumental structures, paintings and sculptures available for general appreciation. The peripheral areas in a few cases complement the older centre, but are often clearly inferior, less inviting and more depressing. Rather than modify the original urban nuclei to correspond to modern expansions, as was the practice a century ago, today we seek to alter the latter, correcting mistakes and lessening the incongruities with the historic centres.

Many countries have recognized the need to protect historic centres which are now the centres of modern cities. The Council of Europe took up this problem in 1972 and has pursued a consistent policy of encouraging national governments in this regard. The efforts of the president of the Comité des monuments et sites, Alfred Schmidt, is especially notable. The most important theoretical and experimental contributions have come from Italy, where the most renowned and least altered historic centres are found; at the same time, these architectural treasures are threatened by the disorganized development of the second half of the twentieth century described above.

The new tenets adopted in the 1970s and 1980s are the following:

> Recognition of the entire historical centre as a physical organism to protect and restore as a whole. The careful methods designed for the restoration of the historically important structures have to be applied to the 'common' buildings as well. Objectively determined differences of distribution and construction would replace the subjective and controversial idea of value as the criterion of conservation.

> Consideration of the particular nature of the 'treasure' to be conserved. These centres are not inanimate objects to visit like works of art in a museum or the monumental structures in a traditional city, but rather an inhabited setting which possesses those characteristics lacking in modern cities, and demanded once again in this particular historical epoch: a stable relationship between population and the buildingscape, which is to say reconciliation between man and his environment.

The above two points bring out several general aspects of the transformation taking place. The protection of certain special areas had already been included in the better English and Italian plans of the 1950s; it was introduced in a general way in the Netherlands in 1961, in Poland in 1962, and in France by the 1962 Malraux law which created *secteurs sauveguardés*. These measures, however, did not provide sufficient protection from the building that was going on around the protected areas. Development of the suburbs increased rents in the city centres, making more profitable uses necessary and forcing out both inhabitants and traditional trades and property uses. The displaced population naturally migrated to the suburbs, fuelling more growth and intensification of this same process. In order to break this perpetual cycle of maladjustment and stabilize the areas already developed, as well as to plan new settlements, public action will be needed to point out a new direction and establish a series of public and private agreements. Multiple initiatives are badly needed in this area to preserve the multifaceted character embedded in the history of the centres to be saved.

The ambitious goal will be to recognize the 'normality' of the special zones – historical centres previously in equilibrium with their rural surroundings – while seeking instead to isolate the pockets of abnormality represented by the recently constructed suburbs. These latter will then be targeted for eventual reintegration by means of opportune rescue operations. Those values preserved in the historic centres must not only be protected but introduced to unusual surroundings, to the general realm of everyday life, not just that of recreation and free time. And perhaps in a distant future this balance can be reachieved according to Mondrian's prophecy of 1931: 'Beauty in life: this must be more or less possible in the future.'

Experiments of the sort suggested here have so far been sporadic: a few municipal programmes – Bologna (1969–80) and Brescia (1975–90) in Italy; Bamberg in Germany; Amsterdam, Rotterdam and Delft in the Netherlands; Chester and York in Britain – and many other private ones. They seem however to be multiplying as public opinion becomes ever more sensitive to these problems. The link of these projects to a specifically European culture is clear, but in the context of a revived architectural culture, they might serve as models for similar undertakings outside Europe. Analogous experiments are being attempted in the Arab world, South America, India and Japan (where the ground to be made up is greater and the destruction more severe) with the help of Italian, French, British and local architects. At stake is the environment of the human family and not simply of one of its parts, for in today's world none of these parts can consider itself independent.

Reflections on the Future

In the context of imminent economic integration in western Europe and the prospect of new relations with the countries of the east, what will the role of the city be? What new needs, obstacles and problems will arise?

(1)   The cities of Europe represent and in some ways extend the long-run processes, measured in many centuries, that define European history. They symbolize and preserve the late medieval values of local independence against those of the various nationalities developed over the past five centuries. Even those cities that have been national capitals for longer or shorter periods are still first and foremost the capitals of provinces or districts, and maintain an ambiguous relationship with national power, one of both identification and antagonism. Paris and London, long established as the capitals of great powers, are indisputably the most important cities of France and England and maintain today their status as international cities; none the less, in both cases the balance achieved with the rest of the country has been only moderately successful and reveals that the extension of a modern city can be controlled by appropriate measures. The third-ranking European metropolis, Berlin, developed later than Paris and London and was demoted by the division of Germany; its recovery belongs to the future. Madrid – chosen as capital by Philip II in 1561 – Rome and Brussels – made capitals in 1870 and 1830 – are effectively balanced by other Spanish, Italian and Belgian cities of equal importance. In the Netherlands, government functions are actually divided between several cities of the *Randstad*. The Hanseatic cities of Hamburg, Bremen and Lübeck share equal status among the *Länder* of the Federal Republic of Germany. Prague and Vienna, the Habsburg capitals, have been rescaled as the capitals of two small states. The capital cities of the new international organizations – Geneva, Vienna, Strasbourg, Brussels – now compete with those of the national states. In Russia, the traditional competition between the two capitals of Moscow and St Petersburg has yet to be resolved. Only in a few peripheral countries – Greece, Romania, Bulgaria, Portugal – does the capital clearly dominate the secondary cities, as is the case outside Europe.

Throughout Europe, cities house local administrations which continue to carry out the functions of the independent medieval communities, sometimes even within the same boundaries. There are both advantages and disadvantages in this situation. On the one hand, it creates a forum for the debate of restricted and deeply felt political issues, bringing together citizens and administrators; on the other, it impedes the work of those mediating agencies necessary to modern planning, agencies which in some countries, like Italy, simply do not exist. Ecclesiastical organization continues to be modelled on the local community, and the two authorities, civil and religious, confront one another in even the smallest centres, revealing that plurality of community references which characterizes the European tradition.

(2) The cities of Europe form a dense network over a fairly restricted area, the imprint of that crowded world that embarked in the sixteenth century on the conquest of the rest of the globe. The inordinate growth experienced by these cities in the industrial age disrupted the relationship they had till then maintained with the countryside. None the less the countryside remained a precious ideal; reformers like Ruskin, Morris and Geddes lamented its loss, while planners sought its reintroduction into the city by means of public parks.

This relationship is now viewed differently as the entire natural and agricultural environment is in danger. Elsewhere man has only scratched the surface of the vast natural spaces which dominate the cities, and these compensate somewhat for the defects of the urban environment. In Europe it is everywhere apparent that the re-establishment of environmental balance depends not on natural processes but human industry, and in this the city reacquires importance. Reconstruction of a comprehensive environment begins in the historic centres – rather than in the countryside – which survive as a model of a balanced and ordered setting of human dimensions. The seemingly densest cities – Venice, Bologna, Bruges, Prague – are in fact tightly bound worlds of buildings, parks and water, punctuated with direct and inspiring openings to the protected open spaces in their immediate vicinity.

The city is at once the laboratory of environmental reconstruction and the guarantee that an undertaking of this sort is feasible, providing that the particular city dates from the not too remote past and continues at least partially to function.

(3) The isolation of cultural treasures in the protected sphere of the museum and of entertainment – the separation of beauty from life perceived by the Neoplastic painters – becomes an ever greater threat as the means of mass communication expand the sphere of entertainment and increase the passivity of its consumers.

The permeable filter of façades separating public and private spaces in the pre-industrial European city provides the means for a different distribution and use of these treasures. Images accumulated over a long stretch of time form the backdrop to life, work and simply getting from one place to another. The contemplation of beauty finds a place in the daily course of one's life rather than as an experience specifically reserved for leisure hours.

Today this need is increasingly filled by modern means of communication lacking specific links in time and space. The images of painting, sculpture, and architecture, not to mention visual and audio performances, are spread by means of books, magazines, newspaper supplements, television, discs and cassettes in a way that eliminates direct contact and hampers independent judgement. We learn that an Impressionist painting has been purchased by a Japanese collector for an astronomical sum and wonder where the work will end up, presumably in the reinforced vaults of a bank.

The city, in so far as it continues to function, remains a real alternative to these processes and points out their shortcomings. While the market for reproduced images excites progressively less interest, people flock to art exhibitions to view the original works, and travel to visit them in their original sites. We learn, however, to appreciate these works better if we encounter them in the course of our life and work, alternating between their enjoyment and our daily thoughts; the environment itself becomes a real work of art which we can enter and in which we can live, and the single works become the elements that make up this environment and not simply random images. There is a great difference between living, working and getting about in a pleasant as opposed to an unpleasant environment.

In other continents where the cities are farther apart and less intensely linked to memories of the past, the images provided by the mass media are often the only ones available, highlighting the need to expand the human compass of the city beyond its traditional limits of time and space. This will perhaps be the central problem of the future. In Europe, the compact physical constellation of large and small cities, though abused and in part passed over by social and political realities, none the less points the way to a responsible and active appreciation of the cultural heritage in its original spatial setting. It also helps to keep the explosion of cultural diffusion under control, standing as a constant point of reference in relation to cultural fads. City management and the intelligence of its managers could play an important role in the contest between the two ways of employing cultural treasures.

(4) The Aristotelian ideal of an integrated environment to be perfected fully to meet human needs regains relevance in today's world. This task was correctly assigned to the open cities of Classical Greece that included the population both within and outside the walls in a physical setting dominated by great, self-sufficient public structures. The European tradition, however, is different. Cities were born as closed entities,[7] in which the need for independence dominated those of internal equality and openness to the outside world. The result was a composite and imperfect setting, formed by a balance of competing forces. We owe much to this tradition: the splendid creations of Venice, Siena, Bruges, Nuremberg and tens of thousands of other centres large and small, each intensely individual, distinguished even from those close at hand; but also the city's political impenetrability, as well as its social and institutional fragility. The quality of urban space depends upon a fluctuating balance between spontaneity and regularity, and upon a combination of public control and private initiative that can either succeed or fail, stimulate creative change or paralyse it.

Urban land rents – income deriving from the semi-permanent leasing of land – were a factor from the beginning, and conditioned the urban landscape from that moment when despotic state power and the associated composition of walled enclosures, like that of the Islamic and oriental cities, began its decline. In the mercantile cities of medieval and Baroque Europe – Genoa, Florence, Antwerp, Amsterdam – property speculation was not abolished but inscribed within pre-established limits. In fact, speculative competition almost always served to complement the uniform pattern imposed by public design, adding an unforced random quality. The expansion of Amsterdam along the three semicircular canals planned by Staets in 1607 can be compared to Jordaan's suburb in which the urban design derives automatically from the speculative parcelling of land according to no particular plan.

These limits were exceeded one and a half centuries ago when Prefect Haussmann lost in his confrontation with the president of the State Council, Baroche, as described in chapter 6. This outcome exacted an enormous price in terms of economic and spatial balance; from that date property speculation exerted an excessive influence on urban transformations. The remedy, however, was not the permanent public management of the entire urban terrain, a solution incompatible with the European tradition and one which led to disastrous results in socialist eastern Europe. What was needed instead was the re-establishment of an appropriate degree of competition between public and private interests. It is a problem of degree, like many other of the problems associated with the European tradition.

The new combination of public and private interests proposed in the first decades of the twentieth century operates along chronological as opposed to spatial lines; it calls for public intervention at those moments when the urban fabric undergoes change, while giving free rein to private initiative in the intervening periods. It is the best proposal to date for re-establishing, within the new social and institutional context, that balance between the two spheres which had always characterized European history, and for reintroducing qualitative invention to the various scales of planning. The dominance of public or private decision-making is not at issue here, but instead their correct placement in a process which succeeds in maintaining both orderliness and spontaneity.

In a global context, the three urban planning models devised in Europe after the Middle Ages, the geometric grid for new settlements built from the sixteenth century onwards, and the two procedures for modernizing existing settlements in the second half of the nineteenth century and the first third of the twentieth, coexist in all parts of the world. The grid predominates where the initial process of settlement is still going on, while the two others apply specially to the transformation of more densely populated areas. In the United States, for example, the sequence of events I have described, was largely avoided: conflict with the industrialized environment was softened by the multiplicity of alternatives available in so vast a territory and by the existence of areas reserved for many different public uses. Generally speaking, the more recent models, however, share the goal of accommodating different scales of planning and a variety of competing decisions within a complete and rational plan entrusted to the public administration. The most extraordinary urban setting in the world, that of Manhattan, was produced by the vertical competition of an infinitely diverse set of structures, all taking off from the uniform grid planned in 1811. It is the last and most sensational product of the imperfect research that characterizes the European tradition, and seems to be, in these general terms, inseparable from a democratic system. In order to follow up on the Aristotelian ideal of a *human* city, the only way left open remains that of gradual, perfectible (and as yet unachieved) mediation.

We should recognize at once the historical and novel aspects of this undertaking. Even in Europe, where there exists such a portentous heritage of historical urban settings, it is pointless to consider reproducing the methods and forms of a past long superseded. The integrity of a humanized environment – city and countryside – are no longer guaranteed by tradition, but entrusted instead to critical opinion which must continually revise and correct itself. The two methods of urbanization developed after the break with the *ancien régime* today confront one another and the outcome is still far from clear.

Preservation of the architectural heritage turns on this debate as well and transcends our present-day concerns by its inclusion of future generations, probably better equipped than we to understand and utilize these assets. The preservation of inanimate objects can be accomplished by means of restoration and protection in a museum; the preservation of the city, however, requires the

92   Venice: 'acqua alta', 1966 (photo: UNESCO).

re-establishment of equilibrium between interests in the decision-making process so that the physical setting and the social body can also achieve a balanced coexistence.

The unresolved situation of Venice is emblematic. The uniqueness of the Venetian setting – water replacing land, no automobiles – sufficed to bring about its functional marginalization which might have easily been countered using the tools of modern technology. Instead, external speculative interests, which profit by the city's decay and are more powerful than both the combined interests of the Venetian population and world opinion, have ensured that this situation continues and worsens. Neither money nor means are lacking, but perhaps so famous a spot, in the heart of civilized Europe, cannot be salvaged as a functioning city and will become instead an inanimate setting, made part of the sphere of free time, of tourism, of the inverted-commas sort of 'culture'.

This problem is one that concerns not only Europe, but the entire modern world. In his *New Industrial State* of 1967, Galbraith asked why our society had failed to create a harmonious physical setting and suggested three possible reasons: insistence on productivity, the vertical limitation and unlimited horizontal expansion of the environment, and the collective rather than individual nature of environmental decisions.[8] Today's unbalanced cities are an indication that something in the modern world is not as it should be. But the cities of Europe, not yet entirely unbalanced, show that the creation of a harmonious environment is possible and so make the utopian ideal of an improved – or at least not worsened – physical setting for modern society seem less improbable.

Notes

Notes to the Introduction

1 C. Baudelaire, *Les Fleurs du mal* (Paris, 1957 [1861]), CVI, 'Le cygne', pp. 240–2. Translation here is from C. Baudelaire *Les Fleurs du Mal: The complete text of The Flowers of Evil*, transl. Richard Howard (Pan Books, 1987), 'The Swan', pp. 90–1.

Old Paris is gone (no human heart
changes half so fast as a city's face)
. . .

Paris changes . . . But in sadness like mine
nothing stirs – new buildings, old
neighborhoods turn to allegory,
and memories weigh more than stone.

2 H. Pirenne, *Medieval Cities* (Princeton, 1925).

Notes to chapter 1

1 St Ambrose, *Lettere = epistulae* (Milan, 1988).
2 St Augustine, *The City of God* (New York, 1983 [426]).
3 Sumerian inscription cited in H. Uhlig, *Die Sumerer* (Munich, 1976), ch. 1.
4 Aristotle, *The Politics* (Cambridge, 1988), pp. 1–4.
5 R. Lopez, *The Birth of Europe* (New York, 1976), p. 15.
6 Tertullian, *De spectaculis*, ed. J. P. Migne, *Patrologia Latina*, vol. 1, (Paris, 1866), col. 720.
7 E. Ennen, *The Medieval Town* (Amsterdam, 1979), p. 46.

Notes to chapter 2

1 Ibn Hawqal, quoted in L. Di Mauro, *Guida ai centri minori del TCI*, vol. 3 (Milan, 1985), p. 55.
2 Sabellico (M. Cocci), *Rerum venetarum ab urbe condita* (Venice, 1487).
3 F. Sansovino, *Venetia* (Venice, 1581).
4 Le Corbusier, *Cahiers*, 4 June 1934.
5 Personal communication to the author from Professor G. De Angelis d'Ossat.
6 V. Franchetti-Pardo, *Storia dell'urbanistica dal Trecento al Quattrocento* (Rome–Bari, 1982), p. 197.
7 This expression is taken from C. Orwell and J. L. Waldhorn, *A Gift to the Street* (San Francisco, 1976).
8 Y. Renouard, *Les Villes d'Italie de la fin du Xe siècle au début du XIVe siècle*, 14 vols (Paris, 1961–5), vol. 2, p. 65.
9 A. Morgado, *Historia de Sevilla* (Seville, 1587), book 1.
10 Pirenne, *Medieval Cities*.
11 P. Lavedan and J. Hugueney, *L'Urbanisme au Moyen Age* (Geneva, 1974), chs 3 and 4.
12 A report of the colloquium appears in M. W. Beresford, *New Towns of the Middle Ages* (London, 1967), ch. 1.
13 R. E. Park, 'The City: Suggestions for the Investigation of Human Behavior in the Urban Environment', in *The City*, ed. R. E. Park, E. W. Burgess and R. D. McKenzie (Chicago, 1925), p. 1.

Notes to chapter 3

1 K. Kyeser, *Bellifortis* (c.1405, Göttingen, Universitätsbibliothek, Cod. phil. 63); 'Manuscript of the Hussite War Engineer' (Munich, Bayerische Staatsbibliothek, Cod. Lat. Monacensis 197), pt. 1; Giovanni da Fontana, *Bellicorum instrumentorum liber* (c.1420, Munich, Bayerische Staatsbibliothek, Cod. icon. 242).
2 F. Braudel, *Civilisation matérielle, économie et capitalisme (XV–XVIII siècle). Les structures du quotidien: le possible et l'impossible* (Paris, 1979).
3 F. Petrarch, *Familiarum rerum libri XXIV* (1325–61).
4 F. Petrarch, *Seniles* (1361–74).
5 E. S. Piccolomini, *Pii II Commentarii rerum memorabilium quae temporibus sui contigerunt* (Vatican City, 1984).
6 J. Huizinga, *The Waning of the Middle Ages* (Harmondsworth, 1972 [1924]), chs 21 and 22.

7 A. Chastel, 'Un épisode de la symbolique urbaine au XVe siècle: Florence et Rome, cités de Dieu', in *Urbanisme et architecture* (Paris, 1954).

8 A. Chastel, *Rénaissance méridionale* (Paris, 1965).

9 G. Manetti's essay is published in L. A. Muratori, *Rerum italicarum scriptores*, III, ii (Città di Castello, 1900–).

10 G. Vasari, *The Lives of the Painters, Sculptors and Architects*, 4 vols (London, 1927 [1550]), vol. 2, pp. 151–5.

11 A. Chastel, *Le Grand Atelier d'Italie* (Paris, 1965).

12 M. Tafuri, *Venezia e il Rinascimento* (Turin, 1985).

13 Filarete (A. Averlino), *Treatise on Architecture* (New Haven, 1965 [1460]).

14 F. Doni, *I mondi* (Venice, 1552–3); F. Patrizi, *La città felice* (1552); L. Agostini, *L'infinito* (1583–90).

15 T. Campanella, Poesie, no. 164, lines 121–2, cited in L. Firpo, *Lo stato ideale della Controriforma* (Bari, 1957), p. 327.

Notes to chapter 4

1 P. Chaunu, 'Introduction générale' in *Histoire économique et sociale du monde*, ed. P. Léon, 6 vols (Paris, 1977), vol. 1, pp. 15–20.

2 I. Wallerstein, *The Modern World-System* (New York, 1976).

3 L. De Camoes, *Os Lusíadas* (1572).

4 G. B. Teràn, *El nacimiento de la America española* (1927).

5 J. H. Parry, *The Age of Reconnaissance* (London, 1962), p. 232.

6 C. Lévi-Strauss, *Tristes tropiques* (New York, 1974), p. 74.

7 Toribio Motolina, *Historia de los indios de la Nueva España* (Mexico City, 1941 [1537]).

8 B. Diaz Del Castillo, *Historia verdadera de la conquista de la Nueva España* (Buenos Aires, 1955 [1568]).

9 A. Ponce, *Relaciòn breve y verdadera de algunas cosas de las muchas suciederan al Padre Fray Alonso Ponce en las provincias de la Nueva España* (Madrid, 1873 [1584]), vol. 1.

10 A. von Humboldt, *Vue des cordillères et monuments des peuples indigènes de l'Amérique* (Paris, 1810).

11 P. Cieza De León, *Cronica del Peru* (London, 1873 [1554]), ch. 35.

12 I. F. Espinosa, *Cronica de la provincia franciscana de los apòstoles San Pedro y San Pablo de Michoacan* (Mexico City, 1945 [1751]).

13 D. Stanislawski, 'Early Spanish Town Planning in the New World', *The Geographical Review*, XXXVII, 1 (1947), p. 96.

14 H. Cortés, cited in F. Guerrero Moctezuma, *Las plazas en las ciudades de la Nueva España* (Mexico City, 1934).

15 *Nuevas Leyes* in Archivio Nacional, Madrid, MS 3017; text in *The Hispanic American Historical Review*, V, 2 (1922), pp. 250–3.

Notes to chapter 5

1 Colbert's note, cited in P. Lavedan, *Histoire de l'urbanisme*, vol. 2 (Paris, 1959), vol. 2, p. 334.
2 C. S. de Montesquieu, *The Persian Letters* (New York, 1929 [1721]), letter 37, p. 69.
3 N. Boileau-Despreaux, *Embarras de Paris*, cited in L. Hautecour, *Histoire de l'architecture classique en France*, 7 vols (Paris 1948), vol. 2, p. 440.
4 J. de La Bruyère, *Caractères* (Paris, 1980 [1688–9]).
5 Letter to Madame de Sévigné, 1 October 1678, in R. Bussy-Rabutin, *Correspondance* (1697).
6 Cited in I. Brown, *London* (London, 1965), p. 94.
7 Ibid., p. 68.
8 L. Knyff and J. Kip, *Le Nouveau Théâtre de la Grande Bretagne* (Amsterdam, 1714).
9 B. Langley, *New Principles of Gardening* (New York, 1982 [1726]).
10 W. Hogarth, *The Analysis of Beauty* (New York, 1973 [1753]).
11 E. Burke, *A Philosophical Enquiry into the Origin of Our Ideas of the Sublime and the Beautiful* (Menston, 1970 [1756]).
12 H. Walpole, *History of the Modern Taste in Gardening* (New York, 1982 [1770–80]).
13 W. Goethe, cited in P. O. Rave, *Gärten der Goethezeit* (Leipzig, 1941), p. 23.

Notes to chapter 6

1 C. Dickens, *A Tale of Two Cities* (Harmondsworth, 1970 [1859]), p. 35.
2 D. Le Roy, *Les Ruines des plus beaux monuments de la Grèce* (1758); J. Stuart and N. Revett, *The Antiquities of Athens* (New York, 1968 [1762]).
3 J. J. Winckelmann, *History of Ancient Art* (New York, 1968 [1764]).
4 E. Chadwick, *A Report on the Sanitary Conditions of the Labouring Population of Great Britain* (London, 1842); F. Engels, *The Condition of the Working Class in England* (Oxford, 1958 [1845]); L. R. Villermé, *Tableau de l'état physique et moral des ouvriers* (Paris, 1979 [1840]); J. A. Blanqui, *Des classes ouvrières en France pendant l'année 1848* (Paris, 1979 [1849]).

5 H. Heine, *English Fragments* [1828] in *The Works of Heinrich Heine*, 12 vols (New York, 1906), vol. 3, pp. 344–8.

6 R. Owen, 'Report to the Committee for the Relief of the Manufacturing Poor, March 1817', in *A New View of Society and Other Writings* (London, 1927); C. Fourier, *Traité de l'association domestique-agricole* (Paris, 1822); C. Fourier, *Nouveau monde industriel et sociétaire* (Paris, 1971 [1829–30]); F. Engels, *The Housing Question* (New York, 1935 [1872]).

7 Article from *The Economist* cited in J. H. Clapham, *An Economic History of Modern Britain*, 3 vols (Cambridge 1950), vol. 1, p. 545.

8 The text of the 1850 French law can be found in L. Benevolo, *Le origini dell'urbanistica moderna* (Bari, 1963).

9 The discussion of Haussmann is cited in G.-N. Lameyre, *Haussmann 'préfet de Paris'* (Paris, 1958), p. 19.

10 G. E. Haussmann, *Mémoires*, 3 vols (Paris, 1890), vol. 2, pp. 310–11.

11 Ibid., pp. 311–12.

12 E. and J. de Goncourt, *Journal* (18 November 1860) (Paris, 1956); P. J. Proudhon, 'La capacité politique', cited in E. Dolléans, *Histoire du mouvement ouvrier* (Paris, 1939), vol. 1; A. Delvau, 'Les Heures parisiennes' (Paris, 1882 [1866]); V. Sardou, *Maison neuve* (Vaudeville, 4 December 1866) (Paris 1867), act I, scene 12.

13 L. Blanc, A. Picard and H. K. B. von Moltke, cited in Lameyre, *Haussmann 'préfet de Paris'*, p. 285.

14 M. du Camp, *Recollections of a Literary Life*, 2 vols (London, 1893), vol. 2, p. 300.

15 G. Doré and B. Jerrold, *London, a Pilgrimage* (London, 1872).

16 R. Baumeister, *Städterweiterung in technischer baupolizeilicher und wirtschaftlicher Beziehung* (Berlin, 1876); J. Stübben, *Der Städtebau* (Darmstadt, 1890); R. Unwin, *Town Planning in Practice* (London, 1909).

Notes to chapter 7

1 J. F. C. Turner, *Housing by People* (London, 1976); C. Abrams, *Housing in the Modern World: Man's Struggle for Shelter in an Urbanizing World* (Cambridge Mass.,1964); G. K. Payne, *Urban Housing in the Third World* (London, 1977).

2 C. Baudelaire, *Les Fleurs du mal* (Paris, 1957 [1861]), CXXII, 'Rêve parisien', p. 281. Translation here is from C. Baudelaire *Les Fleurs du Mal: The complete text of The Flowers of Evil*, transl. Richard Howard (Pan Books, 1987), 'Parisian Dream', p. 106.

Sleep is full of miracles!
 Some impulse in my dream
had rid the region I devised
 of every growing thing,

and proud of the resulting scene
 I savored in my art
the rapturous monotony
 of metal, water, stone . . .

3 Ibid., CL, 'Le voyage', p. 371. Translation 'Deep in the Unknown to find the *new*!' in ibid., 'Travelers', p. 157.
4 W. Kandinski, 'Die kahle Wand', in *Die Kunstnarr* (Dessau, 1929).
5 P. Mondrian in *De Stijl* (March and May 1922); P. Mondrian, 'Pure Plastic Art' [1942] in *Plastic Art and Pure Plastic Art* (New York, 1945), p. 32.
6 F. Osborn and A. Whittick, *New Towns* (London, 1963).
7 M. Weber, *Die Stadt* (1921).
8 J. K. Galbraith, *The New Industrial State* (London, 1967).

Bibliography

The present work explores the history of the European city endowed with a specific identity connected with that of Europe as a whole; it is an argument that has rarely received independent treatment. It is, however, an argument that bears relationships to many other broader subjects – the city in general, the physical form of the city, and related temporal and spatial events – for which there exists a vast literature. Moreover, any broad study of the city, whatever its point of view, presupposes a large, and in the case of Europe, very large, number of studies on individual cities.

The general concept of the city has been a feature of European culture from its earliest beginnings. As a historical problem, however, it has been studied only in the recent past. Important from several points of view are the following:

M. Weber, *Die Stadt* (Munich, 1921).

R. E. Park, 'The City: Suggestions for the Investigation of Human Behavior in the Urban Environment', in R. E. Park, E. W. Burgess and R. D. Mckenzie, eds, *The City* (Chicago, 1925).

V. G. Childe, *Social Evolution* (London, 1956).

P. Sjoberg, *The Preindustrial City* (Glencoe, 1960).

A. Toynbee, *Cities on the Move* (London, 1970).

P. Bairoch, *Cities and Economic Development* (Chicago, 1988).

Literature on the city as a physical organism has developed in tandem with modern urban planning. There are many works treating the historical evolution of the city throughout the world, of which we cite:

P. Lavedan, *Histoire de l'urbanisme*, 2nd edn, 3 vols (Paris, 1952–66).

L. Mumford, *The City in History* (New York, 1961).

C. Stewart, *A Prospect of Cities* (London, 1952).

F. R. Hiorns, *Town-Building in History* (London, 1956).

E. Egli, *Geschichte des Städtebaues*, 3 vols (Erlenbach–Zurich, 1959–67).

G. Burke, *Towns in the Making* (Norwich, 1971).

A. E. J. Morris, *History of Urban Form* (London, 1972).

L. Benevolo, *History of the City* (Cambridge, 1980).

Among the more systematic non-historical treatments we note:

E. N. Bacon, *Design of Cities* (London, 1957).

S. Kostof, *The City Shaped* (London, 1991).

There are several works on the cities of Europe as historical realities and physical organisms which stop at the medieval period:

Henri Pirenne, *Medieval Cities* (Princeton, 1925).

F. Rörig, *The Medieval Town* (Berkeley, 1967).

E. Ennen, *The Medieval Town* (Amsterdam, 1979) (with a large general bibliography).

The following period, from the Renaissance on, has not been dealt with in any similar work, but only in several general treatments:

W. Braunfels, *Urban Design in Western Europe: Regime and Architecture 900–1900* (Chicago, 1988).

P. M. Hohenberg and L. Hollen Lees, *The Making of Urban Europe, 1000–1950* (Harvard, 1985).

R. E. Dickinson, *The West European City* (London, 1961).

There comes then the sea of works on individual regions or periods in European urban history. Among the most important of these are:

E. A. Gutkind, *International History of City Development* (New York, 1964–72). This series consists of eight volumes, all dealing with Europe: vol. 1, *Urban Development in Central Europe;* vol. 2, *Urban Development in the Alpine and Scandinavian Countries;* vol. 3, *Urban Development in Southern Europe: Spain and Portugal;* vol. 4, *Urban Development in Southern Europe: Italy and Greece;* vol. 5, *Urban Development in Western Europe: France and Belgium;* vol. 6, *Urban Development in Western Europe: The Netherlands and Great Britain;* vol. 7, *Urban Development in East-Central Europe: Poland, Czechoslovakia and Hungary;* vol. 8, *Urban Development in Eastern Europe: Romania and the USSR.*

K. Gruber, *Die Gestalt der deutschen Stadt* (Munich, 1983 [1937]).

F. L. Ganshof, *Étude sur le développement des villes entre Loire et Rhin au Moyen Age* (Paris, 1943).

J. M. Lacarra, *El desarrollo urbano de las ciudades de Navarra y Aragon en la Edad Media* (Zaragoza, 1950).

J. Lestocquoy, *Les Villes de Flandre et d'Italie sous le gouvernement des patriciens* (Paris, 1952).

W. Braunfels, *Mittelalterische Stadtbaukunst in der Toskana* (Berlin, 1953).

A. Garcia y Bellido, L. Torres Balbas, L. Cervera, F. Chueca and P. Bidagor, *Resumen historico del urbanismo en España* (Madrid, 1954).

Y. Renouard, *Les Villes d'Italie de la fin du Xe siècle au début du XIVe siècle*, 2 vols (Paris, 1969).

M. Beresfors, *New Towns of the Middle Ages* (London, 1967).

C. Bell and R. Bell, *City Fathers: The Early History of Town Planning in Britain* (London, 1969).

M. Aston and J. Bond, *The Landscape of Towns* (London, 1976) (on England).

G. Duby, ed., *Histoire de la France urbaine*, 5 vols (Paris, 1980–5).

D. Friedman, *Florentine New Towns* (Cambridge, 1988).

In a general work of this sort reference cannot as a rule be made to monographs on single cities. None the less, for their sense of history we cite the following:

J. A. Franca, *Une ville des Lumières, la Lisbonne de Pombal* (Paris, 1965).

A. J. Youngson, *The Making of Classical Edinburgh* (Edinburgh, 1966).

H. Bobek and E. Lichtenberger, *Wien, bauliche Gestalt und Entwicklung seit der Mitte des 19. Jahrhunderts* (Graz–Cologne, 1966).

J. Haddon, *Bath* (London, 1973).

G. Pfeiffer and W. Schwemmer, *Geschichte Nürnbergs in Bilddokumenten* (Munich, 1970).

On Rome:

I. Insolera, *Roma, immagini e realtà dal X al XX secolo* (Rome–Bari, 1980).

On Paris:

M. Poete, *Une vie de cité, Paris*, 3 vols and an album (Paris, 1924).

L. Bergeron, ed., *Paris, genèse d'un paysage* (Paris, 1989).

On London:

S. E. Rasmussen, *London, the Unique City* (Harmondsworth, 1934).

For the more recent period, since the Industrial Revolution, the literature on European cities mingles with that on the modern city and city planning. Those studies which stand out for historical relevance include:

F. Mancuso, *Le vicende dello zoning* (Milan, 1978).

T. Hall, *Planung europäischer Hauptstädte: zur Entwicklung des Städtebaues im 19. Jh.* (Stockholm, 1986).

On France in the late nineteenth century:

D. H. Pinkney, *Napoleon III and the Rebuilding of Paris* (Princeton, 1958).

A. Sutcliffe, *The Autumn of Central Paris: The Defeat of Town Planning 1850–1970* (London, 1970).

On England:

H. J. Dyos and M. Wolff, eds, *The Victorian City*, 2 vols (London, 1973).

J. T. Coppock and H. C. Prince, *Greater London* (London, 1964)

F. J. Osborn and A. Whittick, *New Towns* (London, 1963).

On the present-day situation:

P. George, *La Ville, le fait urbain à travers le monde* (Paris, 1952).

R. E. Dickinson, *The City Region in Western Europe* (London, 1967).

R. A. French and F. E. Ian Hamilton, eds, *The Socialist City* (Chichester, 1979).

Index

231